P9-DJU-771

Advance Applause

Need a shot of sunlight on a cloudy day? This book's for you. Need a whisper of God's love in a noisy life? You'll hear it as you turn these pages. Need a touch of calm in the midst of chaos? Phil Callaway has provided it here. This book is for all who desire to love God and love life and get confused doing both.

> —**MAX LUCADO,** author of *Gentle Thunder,*
> *Just Like Jesus,* and *When God Whispers Your Name*

Phil Callaway has discovered the key ingredients to a healthy family life—lots of love, lots of faith, and loads of laughter. He packs a double portion of all three in this book. These stories' messages will stay with you even longer than my meatloaf!

> —**MARTHA BOLTON,** Bob Hope staff writer
> and author of *Honey, the Carpet Needs Weeding*

Our lives are parables through which God chooses to speak. Phil Callaway's new book reveals this, out of his own life, and makes the business of listening to your life more than just bearable, but truly joyful. God speaks through the small and ordinary in extraordinary ways. Phil has listened and heard—and thankfully decided to share it with us.

> —**MICHAEL CARD,** author, teacher, and singer/
> songwriter

Keep a copy of this book handy for those times when your three-year-old decides to give the dog a haircut or your baby spits strained squash on your new suit. With insightful wit, Phil Callaway reminds us of the extraordinary wonder of parenthood, on even the most ordinary of days.

> —**ELLEN SANTILLI VAUGHN,** co-author,
> with Charles Colson, of *The Body, Loving God,*
> and *Against the Night*

For many years I have enjoyed reading Phil Callaway's articles in *Servant* magazine. His transparent communication penetrates the heart and gives a lift, a laugh, and a lesson. This book is a great companion for all who participate in this adventure called *family*.

> —**STEVE GREEN,** author and recording artist

Very few authors make me laugh out loud. Phil Callaway makes me roar. Maybe that's why I savor his books like a cup of hot chocolate. Sipping each story slowly, rolling it around my mouth to get the full flavor. Then spitting it all over the room in reaction to the hilarious truth. If you like to enjoy yourself as you are reminded of the beauty of values we have often forgotten, then open your heart, grab your sides and read *I Used to Have Answers, Now I Have Kids.*

—**KEN DAVIS,** comedian, motivational speaker,
and author of *How to Live with Your Kids When
You've Already Lost Your Mind*

Rollicking humor, subtle wit, charm and style don't often coexist in one author's prose, but they surely do in the case of Phil Callaway. In *I Used to Have Answers, Now I Have Kids,* he regales the reader with tales of youth and family life, packed with pleasantries worthy of a Mark Twain. Unlike Twain, however, he also conveys Christian principles in a gentle, unobtrusive manner—never preachy, always apt. Here is reading for great fun—and great values.

—**PAUL L. MAIER,** author of *A Skeleton in
God's Closet* and *Pontius Pilate*

From the moment I picked the book up to the moment I put it down my entire body convulsed with laughter and tears streamed down my cheeks. Some day I shall read it ... Seriously, folks, this is an excellent read. Phil Callaway does a great job of taking everyday experiences, putting a humorous spin to them and then making the reader think. If you enjoy humor that causes you to consider longer than cackle, you'll enjoy Phil's book. Don't buy a copy of this book. Buy a few dozen.

—**JOEL A. FREEMAN,** author of *God Is Not Fair*
and chaplain of the NBA's Washington Wizards

This book could be called *I Used to Be a Perfect Parent—Until I Had Kids!* Phil Callaway has captured the true essence of parenthood. It is so refreshing to read a book by a real parent with real kids. This is my kind of book—easy to read, down-home humor and illustrations that mirror family life in today's home. Phil doesn't preach, but his light, easy style will lovingly challenge you to be the parent you really want to be. Each chapter is a short story that can be read in five minutes. Or you can do what I did and read the whole book in one sitting. You won't want to stop. This is a must-read for every parent, and I don't say that lightly.

—**AL MENCONI,** speaker, author, and president
of Al Menconi Ministries

I Used to Have Answers, Now I Have Kids

Phil Callaway

HARVEST HOUSE PUBLISHERS
Eugene, Oregon 97402

Some of these stories have been adapted from Phil Callaway's *Daddy, I Blew Up the Shed* (Harvest House, 1994) and *Honey, I Dunked the Kids* (Harvest House, 1993).

All Scripture quotations are taken from the Holy Bible: New International Version®. NIV®. Copyright © 1973, 1978, 1984 by the International Bible Society. Used by permission of Zondervan Publishing House. The "NIV" and "New International Version" trademarks are registered in the United States Patent and Trademark Office by International Bible Society.

Cover by Terry Dugan Associates, Minneapolis, Minnesota

I USED TO HAVE ANSWERS, NOW I HAVE KIDS

Copyright © 2000 by Phil Callaway
Published by Harvest House Publishers
Eugene, Oregon 97402

Library of Congress Cataloging-in-Publication Data

Callaway, Phil, 1961–
  I used to have answers, now I have kids / Phil Callaway.
    p. cm.
  ISBN 0-7369-0229-5
1. Family—Religious life—Anecdotes. 2. Parenting—Religious aspects—Christianity—
Anecdotes. 3. Callaway, Phil, 1961—Anecdotes. I. Title.
BV4526.2.C245 2000
249—dc21   99-088440
                                                                             CIP

Printed in the United States of America.

00 01 02 03 04 05 06 / BP / 10 9 8 7 6 5 4 3 2 1

For Stephen, Rachael, and Jeffrey.
You've filled my world with laughter,
energy, mischief, and love.
I'd trade you kids for answers any day.

Contents

. . . And Then I Had Kids of My Own

"Before I was married I had three theories about raising children.

"Now I have three children and no theories."

—JOHN WILMOT, Earl of Rochester

I USED TO HAVE ANSWERS.

I knew what parents should do with kids who had runny noses. Or short fuses. Or full diapers. I knew what parents should say when kids asked questions like, "Where do babies come from?" and followed them up with, "You're kidding! Now tell me the truth!" I knew where they should turn when kids got sick, or broke a vase, or failed third grade. I knew what parents should teach their children about life, liberty, and the pursuit of stuff. I knew what time to send them to bed. When to allow them to speak.

And then I had kids of my own.

Three of them.

In three short years.

I soon discovered that parenting is the biggest investment we will ever make, yet children come with no instruction manuals, no "mute" buttons, and no guarantees. And if we happen to have all the answers with our first few kids, chances are that God will send along a little surprise package who will change everything. Chances are this same child will go to Bible camp one day and send us a letter which causes us to question every answer we've ever had:

Dear Mom and Dad,

Our camp counselor told us to write our parents in case you heard about the flood and got worried. Don't worry, we're fine. I got out of the cabin just before it floated away, and I still have my toothbrush. Nobody got drowned because most of the kids were out in the woods looking for Isaac. Luckily black bears aren't as fierce as grizzlies, so Isaac is okay. Please call his mom and tell her. He can't write because of the cast. We never would have found him in the dark if it hadn't been for the lightning.

Did you know that if you put a gas can on a fire, it will blow up? Wet wood doesn't burn so good, but tents do. And clothes. Billy is going to look weird until his hair grows back. We'll be home Saturday if Mr. Chadwick gets the van fixed. It wasn't his fault about the accident. The brakes worked fine when we left. It's a neat van. He doesn't need insurance on it. And we can get it dirty or ride on the roof. It gets pretty crowded up there with 15 kids.

Mr. Chadwick is cool. He's gonna teach me how to drive. Don't worry, he only lets me drive on mountain roads where there isn't much traffic. Just logging trucks and moose. Tonight he's gonna teach me to swim. And dive off the rocks.

I threw up this morning. Our speaker, Mr. Gibbs, said it was probably just the leftover potato salad. He says he used to get sick like that on the food in prison. I'm so glad he got out and came to teach us about the Bible. Well, I better go. We're going to town to mail these letters and buy bullets. Don't worry about a thing.

Love, Jimmy

PS: How long since I had a tetanus shot?

Although we parents may not have as many answers as we once did, there's one thing we'll never be short on: stories. For almost a decade I've been telling the stories you are about to read to audiences around the country. I have watched people laugh (two have fallen off chairs) and I have watched them cry. I have watched couples—who struggle with the challenges that face us all—smile with renewed hope for their kids. And they've told me why: "I've seen my family reflected in yours. And if there's hope for you, Phil, there's hope for anybody."

I'm not quite sure what they meant, but perhaps you'll agree with them.

What you are about to read is a collection of short stories. Stories of mischief, laughter, and hope. Stories that will remind us that even at the worst of times, the best is coming. If you read between the lines, you'll hear the voice of a man who can't thank God enough for his family. For three children who have drained his pocketbook and filled his heart. And a wife who loves him even though his hair is blowing in the breeze and he hasn't the energy to chase after it.

May you find your family reflected in these pages. And should you have half as much fun reading these stories as I have telling them, then I think that we shall both be happy.

Phil Callaway
Alberta, Canada

The Early Daze

Like most parents I know, I was unprepared for
parenthood. For runny noses, and early mornings,
and tripping over toys in the dark. I wasn't prepared
for changing diapers and heating bottles and mashing
peas. And so I let my wife do these things. Just kidding.
Like most guys of my era, I sat through prenatal
class, learning how to breathe and watching R-rated
films. I read all the right books, highlighting applicable
portions and reading them twice. Still nothing quite
prepares you for kids who gouge your car, push
jam in your stereo, then reach up with sticky
hands and say, "I love you, Babs." I had no
idea how quickly three children would change
my life. And how much we can learn when
we embrace life's little surprises.

1

Three-Foot Burglar

IT IS MIDNIGHT. In the Western Hemisphere children are sleeping. Lullabies have been sung. Prayers said. I am just settling down for a short winter's nap when down the hall comes the sound of muffled footsteps. Slowly they draw near.

Burglars?

In that no-man's land between consciousness and sleep, the worst becomes the possible. I am wide awake, my heart thumping wildly. Do I dial 911? Or hit the light switch?

Silently our door swings open.

In the soft glow of a nightlight stands a lone figure. He is about three feet tall and smiling around his soother. His name is Jeffrey Paul. A pillow hangs limply from his left hand, and from his right: a pail of Lego blocks. For a two-year-old who can't spell "schedule," it is time to play.

"Come," I whisper.

Setting down the pail, he clutches the pillow and climbs in. Putting one arm across my chest, he lets out an excited squeak.

"Daddy, I afwaid," he says.

Ah, Jeff, I wouldn't trade you for all the beans in Boston. But, I'm ashamed to say, it wasn't always this way . . .

Three years ago. September 30. Location: the dinner table.

"Honey, I think . . . um . . . well I think I just might be . . . uh, *pregnant.*" My wife was talking with my mouth full. Resisting a choking reflex, I took a quick drink, swallowed the potatoes, and calmly responded, "WHAT? THAT'S IMPOSSIBLE! RACHAEL IS THREE DAYS OLD!"

"Three *months* old," she corrected me.

"But it can't be. You're joking, aren't you? Ha, you're joking." I looked at her closely. She wasn't joking. Husbands know these things.

"I was just starting to feel like I could get up in the morning. . . ." Her words were distant. I stabbed another potato. Hard. "Three kids in three years!" Her words were getting closer. "And I was looking forward to some things: sleep, peace—even holidays."

Nine months later. Location: maternity ward, local hospital.

Gathered with us to witness this most private of events were the obstetrician, the pediatrician, the anesthesiologist, the janitor, the janitor's understudy, the taxi driver, and three pre-med students. But we really didn't notice. You see, Jeffrey Paul had just been born. He came into the world much like our other two, but you didn't need a grade-eight education to determine he would be very different. From week one Jeffrey let us know, long into the night, that he was not pleased to be here. No, this was not his decision, and someone else should pay.

His whimper could melt your heart, but his piercing howl could peel wallpaper. "He's colicky," explained my wife. "I was when I was his age, and your mother says you were, too." Having access to this information did not help.

By the time he learned to use a pacifier, another problem had arisen: Jeffrey was—well—aggressive. Some would call him strong-willed. Impossible even. If he wanted something, he would stop a parade to get it. This became frighteningly evident long before the day we stood in a cafeteria line and watched him reach out and punch a total stranger—perhaps for the sheer joy of watching her bend over to rub her knee.

"Do you suppose we got the wrong one?" I ventured that night. "You know, sometimes the baskets get swapped."

"Naw," my wife responded. "He's too much like you."

She was right.

Born of parents who were beginning to resemble Abraham and Sarah (Mom and Dad cashed old-age pension checks to pay my maternity bills), I was politely referred to as the caboose. An afterthought, said some. A mistake, said my high school teachers. But I never heard those words from Mom and Dad. Instead, I heard words like "I love you" and "I don't know what I would do without you." And, just as importantly, I was shown that love. I was loved, just like the rest.

And so, little Jeffrey, it will be with you. Not because it's all I know, or because it's the noble thing. But because God's grace always accompanies life's surprises. And because it's true: I can't imagine life without you. Life without your "Wock me, Dad." Life without your smile.

But now it's time for bed. Jeffrey picks up his Lego blocks. I gather his pillow, and we head for the crib. "Goodnight, Jeff, I love you."

"Lub you, too," he says. *Ah, these are great days.*

Though I do not know it yet, this boy will turn out to be one of God's greatest gifts to me. In years to come, Jeffrey will greet me at the door like a playful puppy, removing the agony of a stress-filled day with a simple laugh. In years to come he will provide me with a joyful, action-packed reminder that God knows what He's doing. And that He gives His best gifts where He finds the vessels empty enough to receive them.

Back in bed I drift off again, when down the hall comes the sound of muffled footsteps. Slowly they draw near. Burglars? I don't think so.

CHAPTER

2

The Bare Witness

It's BATH NIGHT. Around the world hurried and harried parents seize precious moments to rest and recharge while their children set uncontested Olympic records in the dunking and I-got-more-water-on-the-walls-and-ceiling-than-you-did events.

At our peculiar house, on this particular night, a four-year-old and his younger brother are all wet. The older is constructing a bubble bath beard on the younger. I can't help overhearing their conversation . . .

"Did you know that you've done bad things?"

"Ya." It is one of three words one-year-old Jeffrey knows. The other two are "Yep" and "Uh huh."

"You have done sins," continues the four-year-old kindly.

"Yep."

"And you shall go to hell."

"Yep."

"Hell is hot."

The one-year-old is making a hole in the soap bar.

19

"But you can go to heaven. Do you want to go to heaven?"

Jeffrey sips some bath water before responding: "Uh huh."

"Then ask Jesus into your heart."

"Yeah."

"I'll pray for you, okay?"

"Yep. . . ."

Moments later an excited four-year-old stands before his parents dripping wet, wearing . . . a smile. "Daddy! Mommy! Guess what?"

"What, Stephen?"

"Jeffrey asked Jesus into his heart."

Jeffrey is one. You might say that he's a baby Christian.

"Rachael!" A few days have passed since Stephen claimed his first trophy. He is on a roll, and he isn't about to stop now. Especially at mealtime. "Did you know that you've done bad things?"

"No." It is two-year-old Rachael's most common response.

"You have done sins," the four-year-old continues, undaunted.

"Haven't." Rachael is trying to stab a pea with a fork.

"Yes, you have."

"No. Haven't . . ."

"YES!"

"NO!"

"YEEEEEESSS YOU HAVE!" The witnesser throws part of a sesame seed bun at the witnessee. The bun misses. There are sesame seeds everywhere.

"All right, Stephen. Come with me."

Down the hall we go, hand in hand. He is unsure of the consequences. I can't think of a thing to say. Kneeling down, I hold him tight. Ah, my son. The bare witness. "Don't throw things at your sister."

"Okay," he says, and wiggles free. "One more thing," I say, as he disappears around the corner. "You will sweep up those sesame seeds."

Evening has come. The children are tucked in. Mom is out with my VISA card, and I am in bed reading. A little pajama-clad figure with bare feet slowly pokes his head around the corner. "Hi," he says.

"Stephen, you should be asleep." My tone is unconvincing. He knows his father is a softie when it comes to bedtime.

"What are you eating?"

"Grapes."

"Are they good?"

"Come here and see." I pull down the covers and he crawls in. Grapes are better shared.

"What are you reading?" he asks, looking at a book I'm holding. A bestseller. I don't read enough.

"It's the Bible. Do you want me to read to you?"

"Yep."

"I'm reading from a book called Matthew. Remember the song you like, 'I don't wanna be a Pharisee, 'cause they're not fair you see . . . ?' Well, one of the Pharisees asked Jesus what He wanted him to do most of all. Do you know what Jesus said?"

"What?"

"He told him to love God with everything he had, and do you know what else?"

"What?"

"He told him to love others like he loved himself. Don't you think it's more important to love others than to just tell them about Jesus? You've been telling Rachael and Jeffrey about Jesus, and that makes me glad. But they need to see how kind you are to them before they'll believe what you say about Jesus. Love them, Stephen. Grown-up Christians like to talk about *contacts* and *souls.* Sometimes we sort of throw buns, too, but we don't talk very often about loving those who don't know Jesus. We need to love people until they ask us why."

My son has been silent. Undoubtedly he is impressed with my verbose rhetoric. I mean, let's face it. This has been pretty good stuff. I look over at him. His mouth is wide open, but not with awe. He is sound asleep. Perhaps all this advice was really meant for me.

3

Fork in the Road

I HAVE BEEN A HUSBAND for nearly ten years now, so needless to say I know virtually everything there is to know about my wife's needs. For instance, I know that she can get by without sleep for three days and three nights, but definitely not without chocolate. I also know that she needs flowers, nurturing, romance, protection, a listening ear, clean laundry, and clothes that fit. Whereas, my basic needs are . . . well, pizza.

It is a quarter to five right now and I am sitting at my desk thinking about my need for pizza. It's been one of those days at the office. A computer blip swallowed half the morning's work, and nothing went right after that. I had no time for lunch. Deadlines loom. Reports beckon. And my stomach growls. It is saying, "Hey, give us pizza. We need pizza."

As the clock struggles toward 5 P.M., however, the growling is muffled in visions of home. Dinner will be storebought Coke and homemade pizza. Toppings will include large hunks of pepperoni, layers of ham, and enough cheese to blanket Switzerland. The crust will be light yet crunchy, flavored with a generous pinch of oregano. When I arrive, Ramona will be waiting at the door, her hair permed, her lips pursed. The children will be setting the table, newly washed smiles gracing each of their faces. "Hi Daddy!" they will say in unison. "We sure missed you."

Following dinner, the children will beg to be put to bed early. "We want you and Mom to have some time alone," they will say. "You've probably had a tough day."

As I park the car, however, I realize that something has gone terribly wrong. For one thing, half the neighborhood is in our yard. As I enter the house, I find the other half. They are rifling through our refrigerator. In the kitchen Ramona is bent over the dishwasher, cleaning out the last of the silverware. The table is piled high with laundry, and the stove holds not even a hint of supper.

Several times in my life I have said things people did not appreciate. This is one of those times.

"So what's for supper?" I ask. "Roast beef?"

There is silence.

I sit down before the laundry, and make an even bigger mistake. "So," I say, "what did *you* do today?"

Sometimes my wife moves very quickly. This is one of those times. Ramona stands up straight, brandishing a sharp fork.

"What did I do today?"

She walks swiftly across the room—still holding the fork.

"WHAT DID I DO TODAY?"

She hands me a piece of paper. A piece of paper women everywhere should own. Then she stands over me as I read it.

WHAT I DID TODAY

3:21 A.M.—Woke up. Took Jeffrey to bathroom.

3:31 A.M.—Woke up. Took Jeffrey back to bed.

3:46 A.M.—Got you to quit snoring.

3:49 A.M.—Went to sleep.

5:11 A.M.—Woke up. Took Jeffrey to bathroom.

6:50 A.M.—Alarm went off. Mentally reviewed all I had to do today.

7:00 A.M.—Alarm went off.

7:10 A.M.—Alarm went off. Contemplated doing something violent to alarm clock.

7:19 A.M.—Got up. Got dressed. Made bed. Warned Stephen.

7:20 A.M.—Warned Stephen.

7:21 A.M.—Spanked Stephen. Held Stephen. Prayed with Stephen.

7:29 A.M.—Fed boys a breakfast consisting of Cheerios, orange juice, and something that resembled toast. Scolded Jeffrey for mixing them.

7:35 A.M.—Woke Rachael.

7:48 A.M.—Had devotions.

7:49 A.M.—Made Stephen's lunch. Tried to answer Jeffrey's question "Why does God need people?" Warned Stephen.

8:01 A.M.—Woke Rachael.

8:02 A.M.—Started laundry.

8:03 A.M.—Took rocks out of washing machine.

8:04 A.M.—Started laundry.

8:13 A.M.—Planned grocery list. Tried to answer Jeffrey's question "Why do we need God?"

8:29 A.M.—Woke Rachael (third time).

8:30 A.M.—Helped Stephen with homework.

8:31 A.M.—Sent Stephen to school. Told him to remember his lunch.

8:32 A.M.—Had breakfast with Rachael. Porridge.

Rest of morning—Took Stephen's lunch to him. Returned library books. Explained why a cover was missing. Mailed letters. Bought groceries. Shut TV off. Planned birthday party. Cleaned house. Wiped noses. Wiped windows. Wiped bottoms. Shut TV off. Cleaned spaghetti out of carpet. Cut bite marks off the cheese. Made owl-shaped sandwiches.

12:35 P.M.—Put wet clothes in dryer.

12:38 P.M.—Sat down to rest.

12:39 P.M.—Scolded Jeffrey. Helped him put clothes back in dryer.

12:45 P.M.—Agreed to babysit for a friend. Cut tree sap out of Rachael's hair. Regretted babysitting decision. Killed assorted insects. Read to the kids. Clipped ten fingernails. Sent kids outside. Unpacked groceries. Watered plants. Swept floor. Picked watermelon seeds off linoleum. Read to the kids.

3:43 P.M.—Stephen came home. Warned Stephen.

3:46 P.M.—Put Band-Aids on knees. Organized task force to clean kitchen. Cleaned parts of house. Accepted appointment to local committee (secretary said, "You probably have extra time since you don't work"). Tried to answer Rachael's question "Why are boys and girls different?" Listened to a zillion more questions. Answered a few. Cleaned out dishwasher. Briefly considered supper. Briefly considered running away from home.

5:21 P.M.—Husband arrived looking for peace, perfection, and pizza.

I am finished reading now, but Ramona is not through. "Of course, not all my days go this smoothly," she says, still clutching the fork.

"Any questions?"

染染染

Often when Ramona and I are at public gatherings, she is asked The Question: "Do you work?" I'm glad she is not holding a fork at this point. Sometimes I wish she'd say, "Actually I work days, nights, and weekends. How about you?" But she doesn't. She's a kind woman. She practices what I preach. Once, however, she confided that she wishes she had the eloquence to respond as one woman did: "I am socializing three homo sapiens in the dominant values of the Judeo-Christian tradition in order that they might be instruments for the transformation of the social order into the teleologically prescribed utopia inherent in the eschaton."

Then she would ask, "And what is it you do?"

"I'm a lawyer" just isn't all that overpowering after that.

On the day my wife called to inform me that she was pregnant with our first child, we decided (after I picked myself off the floor) to go out and celebrate. That evening between mouthfuls of chocolate cake, Ramona told me that she wanted to quit her job and come home for good. I gulped a little at first. It would cost us half our income, a house of our own, and some Hawaiian vacations, but I don't remember dwelling on it. Instead we celebrated new life. And talked of what we could give, not what we could get. Some of our best friends disagreed with our decision, but we've never regretted it for a moment. Except when we were unable to afford pizza.

When Robert Ingersoll, the notorious skeptic, was in his heyday, two college students went to see him lecture. As they walked down the street afterwards, one said to the other, "Well, I guess he knocked the props out from under Christianity, didn't he?" The other thought for a minute, then replied, "No, I don't think he did. Ingersoll did not explain my mother's life, and until he can explain my mother's life I will stand by my mother's God."

If you are a homemaker, let me encourage you: No one on earth can shape the mind of a child like his or her mother. Yours is the most powerful, most influential role on earth. Abraham Lincoln said, "No one is poor who had a godly mother." He was right. A mother's pay may be poor, but her rewards are out of this world.

Any questions?

4

Starting Out Downhill

"I THINK I'M GOING CRAZY."

It is my wife speaking. From my vantage point—behind a ham and cheese on brown—her voice seems to emanate from a pile of laundry which consists largely of recyclable diapers.

"Why would you want to do that?" I ask. "I know some mothers with *seven* kids who would trade you jobs any day." It is not a good joke. My timing is bad, and the laundry pile does not respond.

I think I know why. Four years ago we enjoyed our last vacation alone. We laughed, talked, slept, and golfed together. But sitting behind the sandwich I feel like we've hardly talked to each other since.

"How about two weeks in the Bahamas?" I say, half joking. "We could borrow the money from your parents." I am no longer joking.

"Well, we need to do something," says the laundry. "I'm as tired as a centipede at a tap-dancing convention."

☿☿☿

That night I make a secret phone call. "Yes," I whisper, "just one night. Think you can handle them that long?"

"No problem," says my mom. "Remember the apron you gave me? 'Grandparents are for lovin' and babysittin'.'"

Twenty-four hours later, we are driving toward the nearest city, not to the airport, but to a hotel with a Great Escape Weekend Rate.

"Will that be a table for two, sir?"

"Yes. Just for two." Ah, it feels good to say the words.

"Smoking or non-smoking?"

"The breathing section, please." Our host is not amused. I should have noticed the blue and white box in his shirt pocket.

Once we are seated, we look around. "This is nice," says Ramona, which being translated meaneth: "I don't see any high chairs. Or bibs. No one is drooling. No one is screaming. Or biting his sister. Just a bunch of adults and a table for two." She is right.

We sit in silence, looking at each other over two yellow roses. I like the way her eyes reflect the candlelight.

"I still can't believe you fell for me," I whisper with a grin.

She smiles.

If the truth were told, it was I who did the falling. We laugh as I begin to recall a very special ski trip seven years earlier. The day I first fell in love. Literally . . .

☿☿☿

If you've ever been foolish enough to try out a ski hill in Canada's Rocky Mountains, you know that, in addition to coaxing both of your skis to go in the same direction, you must face several other obstacles, such as lying on your backside while small children ski past, laughing at you. Some believe that ski poles were designed to help you balance your act. I believe they were designed by someone who was tired of young children skiing swiftly past and needed something to stab them with.

Lake Louise, a "hill" high in the Rockies, was our resort of choice. As I climbed from the car I noticed that it was impossible to see the top of the mountain. For all I knew the chair lift ended in another time zone or even on the moon.

SKIER ONE: "Hey, have you seen Frank?"
SKIER TWO: "Yeah. He went up the lift with Neil Armstrong."

Unfortunately, I am a trusting sort. And so, believing that this many tourists could not be wrong, I followed my potential relatives-in-law toward a long line of eager skiers awaiting The Chair. As I stood at the back of the line, I lost control of my skis and almost activated the insurance policies of a dozen fellow tourists.

It sounds funny now, this domino effect, but I wasn't laughing when they began threatening me with their ski poles.

After brushing myself off and offering my condolences, I climbed awkwardly aboard The Chair. While ascending the mountain, it never occurred to me that, should we ever reach our destination, I had no idea how to disembark. My potential relatives-in-law, and the one I was hoping to impress, had gone on ahead, leaving me to learn by experiment.

"He ice skates pretty good," I heard one of them say. "He shouldn't have much trouble with this."

"SKI TIPS UP," shouted the sign. I put my ski tips up. Then I watched the strangers on either side of me disembark. It looked easy enough. But by the time I had finished admiring their style, the distance to the ground required a bungee cord, and to top it off, the chair was still moving. And so I took the next logical step. Turning around, I let myself slide slowly off and grabbed the front of the chair. From this unique vantage point, I watched the ground on the surface of the moon move farther and farther from my skis.

I sure hope they can shut this thing off, I thought. *If not, this will be a mighty uncomfortable way to ride down the mountain.* As the lift controller began to shout at high decibels words it would be unwise for me to reprint here, I did what people with cords hooked to their legs pay $59.95 to do: I jumped.

It is difficult to say how much time passed before I hit the ground, surrounded by skiers with open mouths.

Then I heard her laugh. How I loved that laugh!

Was it that funny, or was she just glad I was alive? I wasn't sure. In fact, I wasn't quite sure if I *was* alive. But as she came over to help me up, I realized I was falling head over heels in love.

Had I known that I stood a much better chance of getting to the bottom of the hill alive than I did of marrying this girl, I might have changed my mind. But 11 years later, as I reach across the table and take her hand, I am so glad I hadn't.

Ramona takes a flower from the vase and holds it to my nose. Across the room another couple watches us. Suspiciously. Perhaps wondering if we are in the midst of some illicit affair. After all, married people don't act like that, do they?

"It's great to be in love with your wife," I tell her. "And it keeps getting better."

She smiles. "For me, too."

In the early days of our marriage I often wondered if we'd make it this far. Endless arguments. Angry nights when there seemed to be no solution. A clash of wills. Two selfish kids trying to make sense of a lifetime commitment. Marriages are made in heaven, we'd been told. But we learned quickly that they are lived on earth. Looking back now I realize that the one thing neither of us would contemplate was divorce. The word did not enter our vocabulary. Some would say we were stuck with each other. Imprisoned. But I believe it provided us the time, and God the opportunity, to create a better thing between us.

Later that night in the darkness of a quiet hotel room we thank God for His mercy, and I go to sleep with a smile on my face. Things aren't perfect between us, but they're getting better. "It's great being married to your best friend," I whisper, "especially when you start out going downhill."

5

Lady in Blue

I HAVE THE FLU. I think doctors have dubbed it the Shanghai Swine Flu. Symptoms include everything from voice loss to a lack of enough physical stamina to hold up a paperback. These same doctors say the flu will pass, but at the moment—I wish *I* would. Painfully I muster enough energy to reach for the remote control.

One of the joys of small-town living is that our television has snow on almost every channel. Some of the snow is in full color, but mostly it snows in black-and-white. On one of the three channels we receive, the host has just finished his opening tirade and now a kind-faced lady in a blue dress turns toward the camera. "The happiest day in my life," she says, smiling, "will be the day my daughter leaves home. I regretted my decision to have her from day one—you know, the day she was born." Some in the audience heckle. Others applaud. The host excitedly clutches his microphone and runs to the next aisle. His pockets jingle. The phones light up.

I didn't expect to find such encouragement here. But I've finally discovered a few people who are even sicker than I.

The director cuts back to the lady in blue. She is chewing gum now and nervously swinging one leg. I am thinking to myself: *I sure hope her daughter never sees this.*

Incredibly, her daughter is in the audience. Impossible. An eleven-year-old with a two-year-old mother. "My daughter knows how I feel," the lady in blue continues, still smiling, still chewing gum. "We have a very open relationship."

By the time the credits roll, others are beginning to share her sentiments. "Kids are a pain," says one. "They're — like—so much—like—total trouble, you know?" Others agree: "I'd like to get on with my life . . . I was a nurse two years ago; now my career's been put on hold . . . How can I take three steps forward with four kids holding me back?"

One newly married couple shares their incredible insight. "We've watched our friends who have kids, and we've decided that parenthood is too costly. We've decided not to have kids. We'll have things like holidays instead."

Wondering how these folk propose that we continue the human race, I lean over the bed groping for the ice cream bucket, and begin to consider my own situation. I'd be lying if I didn't admit that parenting has its drawbacks. Three kids eat up to 50 percent of a household's income, the statistics tell us. And that's just on Wednesday! However you look at it, children aren't the best financial move you'll ever make. And that's not the end of it. Without children I wouldn't be stepping on Lego land mines after midnight. Or frantically searching for one shoe, a hammer, or the remote control. And just think of the vacations we've missed.

The peace. The quiet. The evenings out. The weekends together—alone.

But a funny thing happened as I rested on my self-pity—the sound of little feet came echoing down the hall. A little boy pressed through the door followed by his little sister. He was holding my dinner at an 18-degree angle. "Here's your first course, Daddy," he said. Toast and butter had never tasted better. A few minutes later he brought me my "final course," sneezed on it, then took his little sister by the hand and went quietly out of the room. The whole thing was obviously choreographed by their mother.

A few nights earlier on the same snowy screen that now lay black before me, Ramona and I had watched Steve Martin's movie "Father of the Bride." While I'm not a fan of some of Steve's characters, his portrayal of George Banks, a father with more trouble than a one-armed coat hanger, had us both laughing, then crying unashamedly. Near the end of the film, George struggles with his daughter's upcoming wedding—the costs, the extravagant reception, and of course, the groom. But as he lies awake through the early hours of the wedding day, memories swirl through his mind like a stroll through a photo album: The day his daughter Annie was born. Her first day of school. Her first bike ride. And finally, the scene which never ceases to turn me into a whimpering father in search of a tall box of Kleenex: Neither dad nor daughter can sleep. They are standing in the driveway where they have played one-on-one basketball through the years. Annie is telling her dad that her stuff is packed, and that she's finding it hard to leave home.

"That's the thing about life," George confesses. "The surprises that sneak up on you and grab hold of you . . . it still happens to me." Annie listens for more, but there's silence. "What is it?" she asks. "It's nothing," says George. Annie wonders if the cost of the wedding is bothering him. "No," he says, "I was just thinking about how I will remember this moment for the rest of my life."

Life is full of moments like that. Moments that make us realize that we are part of a far bigger picture than our own little world. And although I won't be able to tell Sally Jesse Raphael or Jay Leno about the moments that have changed my life forever, none seems more important right now than the memory of a hot May day in 1986 when I first gazed into the eyes of my son. I had seen other babies. They were wrinkled and purple. But this baby was—well—wrinkled and purple, too . . . but truly beautiful. This was my son. Stephen.

We had prayed for this boy. And God answered with the first of three gifts which grow more precious each day. What could be more exciting than watching him grow? Teaching him to ice skate? Showing him how to catch a ball? Or watching him smack a line drive just over my head? How do you put a price tag on the joy I felt the day he suddenly stopped in the midst of a wrestling match, wrapped his arms around my neck, and whispered, "Love you, Daddy."

"Lord, thank You for the privilege of parenthood," I pray. "For these three gifts You have entrusted us with. I give them to You again. Soon these halls will echo only with the memory of their laughter. Help us to make the most of each moment and point them to You each day."

By the way, the flu is gone now. It seems that I passed it on to my wife, and I just sent her dinner—in the hands of a three-year-old.

CHAPTER

6

Superdad's Holiday Adventure

I LEARNED A valuable lesson this week: If evolution were true, mothers would have three hands and an extra set of eyes in the back of their heads.

Last Friday, I was sitting at work, leaning back in my chair, counting the minutes until holidays began. Ah, it would be wonderful! Suddenly my chair back gave way and I hit my head on an old-fashioned radiator that sits in my office just waiting for this to happen.

Although we wouldn't be going far on this vacation (my wife was in the final stages of pregnancy and in a sour mood whenever I mentioned the drive to Alaska), I would finally be able to spend some quantity time with my two preschoolers. I would take them swimming, shopping, to the zoo, to the lake. They would sit and watch me as I worked on the car and cut the grass. They would help me weed the garden. I would even pay them in quarters for their efforts. Ah, vacation! There's nothing quite like it. My lucky wife spent seven days a week at home with these little darlings as

I slaved away near this radiator. Finally, it was my turn to relax.

Things started out pretty well. On our first evening together, I took the kids out for ice cream and they managed to get some in their mouths. But when we arrived home, Ramona informed me that it might be a good idea for us to go to the hospital—RIGHT THIS VERY MINUTE!

I remained perfectly calm. After all, this was not the first time we had gone through this ordeal.

"It's okay, it's okay," I assured her, "I'll be fine."

"Breathe deeply," she said. "Like they taught us in prenatal class."

After seven hours—which rank right up there with barefoot ice fishing—Jeffrey was born. Although I applauded my wife and the miracle of birth, as I drove to pick up our other two angels from their grandparents' house, I wondered again if there wasn't a better way of reproducing. "Certain types of worms merely separate," I said to no one in particular.

That night there was cause for celebration. After the angels were in bed, a friend dropped by to commemorate with me the birth of our third-born. 7-Up, peanuts, and a mediocre movie were the order of the evening, but by the time I went to bed I was thinking, "It's a good thing I'm on holidays. I shall need a little rest."

As I dozed off, visions of summer sun danced through my head. Visions of that trip to the zoo. That boat-ride on the lake. Visions of sipping Coke beneath the maple tree as the children played quietly around my feet.

Suddenly, there he was—pouncing on me.

"Hey Dad, time to get up."

"Whaaat? Where are we? Who are we? Who are *you?* What time is it?"

I groped for the clock. It was 7 A.M. Time for breakfast. After four hours of sleep. I would make the best of it. A meal with the kids. Time to get to know each other. Rachael smiled at me past three teeth. She was so sweet. I pinched her dimple gently. Her pink bib was so clean. Unlike her brother's. Rachael continued to smile at me as she deposited her bowl of soggy Cheerios on the floor. I smiled back. Stephen promptly dropped his piece of bread on the floor, jam side down. "But . . . Daddy," was all he said.

"That's okay."

Then he spilled his milk.

"But . . . Daddy."

By this time I thought we could all use a little fresh air, so off we went—grocery shopping. Now, I must confess that in years past I have been highly critical of supermarket mothers. Especially those with more than one child dangling from their shopping cart squeezing bruises into the peaches. Especially those who have had enough of the screaming and "accidentally" swap carts with other unsuspecting shoppers.

MOTHER: "Have you noticed that flour is $4.99?"

OTHER MOTHER: "I will pay you $499,000 to take my child till Wednesday!"

By the time we reached the checkout counter, I was looking—and feeling—just like one of them.

"What's that hanging from your cart, Mr. Callaway?"

"Oh, that's my eldest child."

"No, no. The red sticky stuff."

On the way home, Rachael remembered that she didn't appreciate being strapped into a car seat. Without a good set of ear plugs a trip to the zoo would be impossible. By nightfall I was exhausted, and I hadn't even done the dishes. Or swept the floor. Or cleaned the house. Or planned breakfast.

The next day dawned early. Again. *Why don't kids just sleep half the morning?* I thought. *I used to when I was in high school.* After another adventuresome breakfast, I put on a children's video and instructed the kids to watch quietly while Daddy rested on the living room floor. It was not a good idea. Fathers in that position should keep their eyes open. Mine were closed. Just as I began to doze off, Rachael brought her soggy diaper to rest on her daddy's head.

Nightfall brought with it the promise of much-needed sleep. But it was not to be. Rachael wouldn't go to sleep. Daddy couldn't find her pacifier. And he was being punished.

I looked everywhere. Twice. Finally I found it in the heat vent. When I brought it to her, she was fast asleep.

"What does Jesus look like?" asked Stephen. *This is not the time. Can't he see Daddy is tired? Questions like this are to be asked after church. Or after a good rest.* I lay down beside him. This was the time for questions at our house.

"When will Mommy come home?"

"Soon," I answered. "Just two more sleeps." Then I began to confess my sins to a three-year-old. "Before I came home for holidays, I thought Mommy's work was easy. But then I saw the mess you two make, and how many diapers need changed. Would you like to make the beds, wash the clothes, make meals, clean the house, change diapers?"

He screwed up his little nose.

"I'm thankful for Mommy," I continued. "I had no idea how hard she works."

He nodded. "She loves Jesus."

"Let's thank Him for her." I prayed out loud asking God's forgiveness for taking my wife for granted, and thanking Him for her hard work. Her unselfish love. Her joyful spirit.

When I looked over at Stephen, he was sound asleep.

And now it was my turn.

On my way to the bedroom I took one last look into Rachael's room. She was standing up in her crib smiling at me past three teeth. And looking for her pacifier.

7

The Fright Before Bedtime

BEDTIME IS STORY TIME at our house. On most nights you will find three children and one father on the couch, sometimes sharing a blanket, sometimes sharing ice cream, but always sharing a book. Our favorites include anything by Dr. Suess, C. S. Lewis, or Stephen King. Okay, I'm kidding about Stephen King. But some people would think the stories I read are worse. After all, almost every night I read the kids *Horror Stories from the Bible*. This is not an actual book (yet) but I must admit that Stephen King could find some plot lines in the Old Testament.

Tonight I have just finished the story in Numbers 16 wherein the ground opens up and the families of Korah, Dathan, and Abiram are—well, let's be honest here— squished. Thankfully the accompanying illustration softens the blow, but according to certain behavioral scientists, this is extremely harmful stuff. Imagine the lasting damage that will be done to the psyches of young, impressionable children. The Bible is violent. It should be banned, they say, in their expensive reports. Then they go home and watch reruns of *The X-Files*.

On this night the behavioral scientists seem to be wrong. Within minutes of the story, and partly due to the serenading of Michael Card's *Sleep Sound in Jesus,* Rachael and Jeffrey have fallen asleep.

But perhaps the scientists would prefer to study Stephen. He is still wide awake and thinking about Korah, Dathan, and Abiram.

"Daddy, tell me the story about the Israel guys again. Could ya? Tell me, 'kay?" Stephen's eyes have every reason to be shut. His light is out. His cassette is on. His head gently rests against a stuffed racoon. But his father is beside him on his favorite chair. "Daddy, tell me about those Israel guys who got swallowed by the dirt."

"Okay. Let's see . . ."

"First tell me about when I was in Mommy's tummy."

"All right. It was about four years ago now. Mommy and I were in bed one night. I was almost asleep when all of a sudden, you kicked me in the back."

"What?" His eyes widen. He lets out a squeak and laughs. It is a story he never tires of hearing. "I kicked you in the back?"

"Yep, and I jumped up and hit my head on the night-stand and stubbed my toe on the bookcase."

"You did?"

"No, but the rest is true. Mommy and I felt her tummy. You kicked some more and we prayed for you just like we had done a hundred other nights. We thanked God for you, Stephen, and we asked Him for a healthy baby. And most of all we prayed that you would grow up to love Jesus."

"Then was I borned?" He is squeezing Mr. 'Coon.

"Not yet. The next thing you did was go to sleep. But Mommy didn't. In fact she didn't sleep at all that night. I made up for it, though. I slept while she paced the floor.

"When she woke me the next morning, I knew it was time to go to the hospital."

"How'd ya know?"

"When Mom says we go to the hospital, we go to the hospital. And you had to go to the hospital, too. You had decided you'd like to see what was going on in the big old world."

"Tell me about the baseball guys."

"Well, when we arrived, I couldn't believe it. There was a baseball tournament going on right across from the hospital. I couldn't believe they would do that. I thought they should all stop playing and pray for us. I mean, a baby was about to be born.

"But that night at 6:04 I held you close and kissed you for the first time, Stephen. Then I put a perfectly formed little baby into Mommy's arms. I'll never understand how she was able to smile after all that, but I've never seen her happier. God had given us a baby boy."

"That was me."

"Yes, that was you. As I stood there, I thought of the many parents who didn't want their babies. And I remembered the verses in the Bible that say, 'You formed me in my mother's body. I praise You because You made me in an amazing and wonderful way . . . You saw my bones being formed as I took shape . . . all the days planned for me were written in Your book before I was one day old.'

"We wanted you Stephen, and we still thank God for you. Every day."

He is smiling again. Both arms surround Mr. 'Coon. "Are you going to work tomorrow?" he asks.

"Yes."

"Then I shall be sad."

"Don't be sad, I'll come back for dinner."

"Will you run away?"

"No, Stephen . . . why did you say that?"

"Some daddies run away."

"Who said?"

"I don't know. Somebody said their daddy ran away and stayed gone."

"No, I won't ever run away. I love Mommy, and I love you kids too much to run away. Good night, Stephen. I love you." I kiss his forehead and stand to leave.

He closes his eyes. "Night," he says.

I move down the hall to check on his sister.

"Daddy?" Stephen is calling again.

"Yes?"

"Is Jesus under my bed?"

"Jesus is with you always, Stephen."

"If Jesus is under my bed, then the woozul can't get me."

"The woozul can't get you. Good night now. It's time to sleep."

"Daddy?"

"Yes, Stephen."

"You forgot to tell me about the Israel guys."

8

False Teeth and Funnybones

PEOPLE OFTEN ASK ME, "Phil, is that your nose or are you eating a banana?" Whoops, wrong question. Let me see. Oh yes, people often ask me, "Phil, where did you get your sense of humor? Did you inherit it and if I pay you enough money may I have it, please?"

Unfortunately, a sense of humor is not for sale. Like poverty and baldness, a sense of humor is hereditary. You get it from your kids. Occasionally you get it from your parents, too. When I was a lad of only eight, I noticed that my dad was a little warped. He could be serious at times of course . . . like when I put nail polish in his lemonade, but mostly Dad was a fun-loving person who believed that those who laugh lots have wrinkles in all the right places when they retire. Dad would have agreed with C. S. Lewis who said, "When I became a man I put away childish things, including the fear of childishness and the desire to be grown up." He thought Billy Sunday was right when he said, "If you have no joy, there's a leak in your Christianity somewhere." I suppose my father worked hard enough to realize the value of play.

I wasn't always thankful for Dad's sense of humor. I remember the time I invited a new kid on the block over to play. I was hoping to impress him, and so it seems was my dad. Though my father still had hair in those days, it grew mostly on one side of his head, something most people didn't realize because he had grown accustomed to combing it over the top. My friend and I were building a log cabin on the living room floor when suddenly he stopped what he was doing and dropped a log on my thumb. "Ouch!" I said, and looking up, found that my friend's mouth was wide open, his eyes agape, his lower lip resting on his new white tennis shoes. He was looking at my father.

Dad, in an effort to imitate someone who was auditioning for the role of Larry in an upcoming Three Stooges film, had just come into the room with his hair hanging down, his eyes crossed, and his false teeth lowered.

Oh no! I thought. *How embarrassing! Dad, how could you?*

I'm sure my friend was thinking: *Help! Aliens! Make a run for it!*

But it was my dad. He dropped to one knee and began tickling me, but my friend drew back, distant and afraid. As he said goodbye that day, I suspected it would be the last time he came to play at the Callaway house. I was wrong. The very next day he was back for more. While playing at his house, I discovered why. At my friend's house, laughter was located under "L" in the dictionary but seldom displayed elsewhere. One night I sat around their dinner table as they read the Bible and prayed, and I remember thinking to myself: *At this house, God frowns.*

Thirty some years have passed. A few months ago my friend, who now lives a few thousand miles away, wrote me. "Brace yourself," he said at the start of one paragraph, "I no longer believe in God." I'm not naïve enough to think he turned his back on God only because his father's funny bone was in a cast. But sometimes I wonder.

By the time my wife and I had three little blessings from above (in as many short years), it became apparent that a sense of humor was more to be desired than baldness on the list of things I had inherited. I believe that when it comes to child-rearing a sense of humor is a serious asset.

Last Sunday afternoon, my son's friend Joel came for a visit and, like all small sensitive boys who realize that Sunday afternoon is for resting and that tired adults may be sleeping soundly, Joel attacked the door with both fists.

ME (after sleepily opening the door): "Hi, Joel. Can I get something for you? Like a hammer?"

JOEL (holding a sharp stick): "Mr. Callaway, can I play with Stephen?"

ME (looking at the stick): "Sure."

JOEL (poking an ant with the stick): "Where is he?"

ME (trying to gently confiscate the stick): "He's up on the roof eating a banana."

JOEL (after backing up to take a look): "I don't see him."

ME: "Well, he'll be down in a minute. You watch. He'll slide down on the peel."

JOEL (dropping the stick and backing onto the road to watch): "I STILL DON'T SEE HIM."

STEPHEN (standing behind me now): "Hi, Joel!"

JOEL (picking up the stick): "Mr. Callaway, you were just joking me."

Of course, this sense of humor thing can be carried too far. My wife gets the biggest laughs out of things that aren't funny at all. Take for instance the day she almost cashed in on my insurance policy.

After a rather tough day at the office, I was looking forward to a peaceful evening at home—changing diapers and playing with three tornadoes. All I had to do was navigate the last turn into our yard while carrying a large black briefcase full of hardback books. I suppose it did not help that I was on a bicycle. Of course you know what happened—my front tire got caught between the lawn and the sidewalk and I was catapulted unceremoniously into the bushes.

It must have looked quite hilarious from the house, because moments later the one who loves me more than life itself stood over me laughing uproariously.

"Are you okay?" she asked as she breathed deeply and tried not to hyperventilate.

"Oh, I'm fine. It's just my right leg." I replied. "The doctor can set it. And the teeth . . . we can get a plate made."

From inside the house, three children were watching our quality time together, their runny little noses pressed up closer to the window pane than to their own faces. "Ha, Daddy funny," one of them said.

I'm not sure how much of this particular brand of humor I want our kids to inherit, but I do know this: A house filled with laughter will never be empty. I pray my kids will remember such a place. When I think back on my childhood, I am forever grateful for parents who passed on the gift of laughter. For a family who taught me to view the funny in the ordinary. To this day, strange though it may seem, I have always found it easier to accept the serious from the lips of the light-hearted.

Perhaps that's why I knelt by my bed when I was just a kid to do something millions of others had done before. I had heard the message of a Savior who loved me enough to die for me. And so I asked Him to be the biggest part of my life. It made perfect sense. You see, I had heard the message from someone I had every reason in the world to believe absolutely. From a mother who felt that the best thing she could do in British Columbia after discovering she had left her false teeth beneath a picnic table near Seattle, Washington . . . was to laugh.

Tales of Mischief

*I don't know about you, but I sometimes worry
about the next generation. A generation raised on
Nintendo and the Spice Girls. When I was a kid,
we didn't have either, and somehow we survived. We
also knew which way to point our hats. And how high to
wear our pants. I grew up in a small town where you
didn't have to go far to find trouble. After chores each
Saturday, my mother told me to go outside and play.
"And be a good boy, Philip." I always obeyed the first
part of her command. My mother may have had some
trouble raising me. But I think she enjoyed it. I met
some interesting people in those days, as you are about to
find out. A genuine saint, who doubled as a school-
teacher. And I learned something from my mother too,
on the day a friend and I invented recycling.*

9

Up in Smoke

I<small>F YOU BUMP INTO</small> the average person on the street, chances are good that they will have heard of recycling (chances are that they will sue you, too, but that's another chapter). Though most humans are familiar with recycling, few know who invented it.

Allow me to set the record straight.

It was the summer of my tenth birthday. A picture-perfect summer, framed with barefoot fishing trips and sleeping beneath the stars. My friend Gary and I established The Gang of Two that summer. I'm not sure if you ever heard of us. But early each morning after our fathers went to work, we borrowed their shovels and spent the day burrowing deep into the bowels of the earth. I, Captain Phil, pretty much gave orders. Private Gary pretty much followed them.

Each day—thanks in large part to Gary's unwavering obedience—we burrowed a little deeper. Each day, by 5 P.M., we returned the shovels to their rightful spots. And no one was the wiser.

As July became August, The Fort became home. Dead tree branches camouflaged her from the onslaught of rival gangs. Tall weeds concealed her inhabitants from passers-by. In those weeds we sat, decked out in imaginary khaki outfits, imaginary guns in hand, launching surprise attacks on passing cars, which were Nazi U-boats and sometimes tanks.

Then one morning in mid-August, after dying theatrically from a U-boat torpedo, Gary spoke the fatal words: "I'm bored."

As captain, it was my job to turn such words into adventure, so I quickly responded, "What say we stop saving The Fort and start saving The Earth?" The thought was a new one for both of us, which was why Gary pushed aside two large flowered weeds, looked at me with his head to one side, and said, "Huh?" But once I explained my plan, it made perfect sense.

That afternoon, as the hot summer sun beat mercilessly through the ozone layer and danced on the asphalt around our feet, we put our plan to work: We purged the main street of our little town of every visible cigarette butt.

GARY (picking up another one): "Boy, are these ever disgusting!"

ME (loudly, in the direction of the curious passers-by): "Yes, Gary. Put 'em in the bag and we'll throw 'em in the trash!"

GARY (with a loathing look): "To think people actually smoke these things!"

Upon completion of our task, we carried the butts to our headquarters in the woods and concluded The Plan: we recycled them, one by one. Right down to the filters.

In fact, we recycled pretty much anything we could get our lips around that summer. Tea leaves. Cinnamon. Dried dandelions. Pencil shavings. Newspaper. Cardboard. You name it, we sat in the weeds and inhaled it.

I believe it was a Wednesday that completely changed our lives. Gary approached me on his bicycle, breathless. "You ain't agonna believe this," he said, throwing himself on the grass, rolling in the suspense of it all.

"Okay, let me guess. Um, it's gotta be candy. Your mom bought you all you can eat?"

"No, better."

"Uh, she bought you a motorcycle?"

"Nope," he said, unable to contain his excitement any longer. "I found A PACK OF 'EM. It ain't even been opened."

"Naw, you're lyin'."

But he wasn't lyin'. In fact, carefully concealed in the tall shadow of an obscure telephone pole was proof: Player's Filter Tip, unopened and beckoning.

Now I knew the punishment for smoking. My older brother had told me all about it. "They cut your lips off," he said. So, casting anxious glances in all directions, we stripped off the plastic and divided The Pack evenly. Ten apiece. And we smoked them. One by one. Right down to the filters.

As our time behind the pole drew to a close, we pooled our wisdom and experience, noting what scientists would later discover: Anything that tastes this bad can't be too good for you. Or, as Gary put it so eloquently, "These things are awful. Let's never ever as long as we both shall live touch another one." After shaking tobacco-stained hands on it, I suggested, somewhat deliriously, that we get home and, furthermore, that we do so quickly, maximizing the time needed to re-enter the non-smoking zone.

"Hmmmm," sniffed Gary's mother. "What's that smell?"

Half an hour had passed, and she was standing outside the family restroom, wondering who had established a tobacco plantation on her property without securing permission. Gary crouched in the bathtub, caught yellow-handed. "I, uh, was smoking," was all he could say. But I was older than Gary. I was wiser. I knew that as ye smoke, so shall ye reek. So, in an effort to keep the consequences of my own sins at bay, I slipped silently through our back door and up to the medicine cabinet. From there, I tiptoed to my room, concealing a can of spray deodorant and a full tube of toothpaste. After lengthy attention to personal hygiene, I was finally able to approach my parents. "Hmmmm," sniffed my father. "You sure smell nice, Philip."

Later that evening I crawled into bed, a satisfied smile stuck to my face. *Boy, are you ever brilliant,* I thought. *No one will ever know.*

Mom entered my room then, opened the window and sat on the bed. "Did it taste good?" she grinned.

"Uh . . . whaa . . . supper? Oh, yes, Mom it was very good. Thank you."

"When I was a girl," she continued, "my grandpa let me smoke his pipe. I didn't like it . . . How about you?"

"Me neither, Mom," I said, closing my eyes. Then I stuck out my lips because I knew the punishment.

She could have cut my lips off. She could have at least spanked me (this had been done before), or quoted Scripture. She could have reminded me that nothing we do will ever be hidden from God. That no amount of toothpaste or deodorant will cover our sins. That they really will find us out. She could have reminded me that the story doesn't end there. That because of what Jesus did on the cross we don't have to hide. That because He paid for our sins we can approach God, forever forgiven.

Instead, she leaned over and kissed me squarely on the forehead.

"I'll never smoke again," I said.

Then, "Mom, how did you know?"

She grinned again. "Well, son, sometimes ten-year-old boys forget that their mothers have friends, too."

From the bathroom my father hollered: "Hey, has anyone seen the toothpaste?"

CHAPTER

10

The Secret

I WAS A SKINNY KID. How skinny, you ask? So skinny I had only one stripe on my pajamas. So skinny I wore snowshoes in the shower to avoid sliding down the drain. I was the only kid on our block who could stand under power lines during rainstorms and stay dry. My fingers were thin, my arms were thin, my teeth were thin. They rushed me to the hospital once. I swallowed a peanut and they thought I was about to have twins.

Okay, enough exaggeration. But it's true: I was woefully thin. And my thinness did not go unnoticed by the other children. "Skinny skinny two by four, slide him under the kitchen door," bullies would chant. I didn't think it was that funny, and once my big brother arrived, I told them so. I also told them things about their ancestry. Things I made up.

When I was nine I discovered hidden within an Archie comic book a full-page advertisement that was destined to change my life forever. It was a Charles Atlas ad. Charles Atlas was the Arnold Schwarzenegger of his day. *Physical Culture* magazine called him the "world's most perfectly developed man." No one chanted slogans when he passed by. Charlie, as I affectionately called him, walked around in Tarzan's body. He could push apes around. He was a handsome, broad-shouldered, thick-chested, slim-waisted man, who wore only leopard-skin trunks. What made the ad so catchy was that Charles Atlas was once like me—a 97-pound weakling. That was, until he found The Secret Formula. A formula which left men envious and reduced beautiful women to lumps of quivering jelly.

The ad showed a puny kid (me) lying on a beach near Miss America. Just when it looked like the weakling might get the girl, a bully ran by and kicked sand in his face, covering him with shame and embarrassment. In the next frame Charles Atlas comes to the rescue: "And to think they used to call me 'skinny,'" he says. "Girls snickered and made fun of me behind my back. Then I discovered my marvelous new muscle-building system. . . . After that, I felt so much better in my big, new, husky body that I decided to devote my whole life to helping other fellows change themselves into perfectly developed men. Give me 15 minutes a day, and I'll give you a new body." Oh yeah. I was sold.

The coming of fourth grade showed me how badly I needed that body. This was the year I first discovered girls. "Wow!" I said to myself during a moment of extraordinary enlightenment, "Girls are . . . different!" To show my deep affection for them, I did what all normal fourth-grade boys do: I began pulling their pigtails.

"You're skinny," said a mean, freckled girl after I finally let go of her red hair. "You're so skinny they can slide you through the keyhole to get the mail."

I was shocked. "Oh yeah?" I retorted. "Well, you're so fat that . . . um . . . that you have to turn sideways to . . . um . . . keep from catching a cold." My words left us both a little bewildered.

It sounds funny now, but when I got home from school that day, I cried.

By eighth grade I had saved enough money to order Charlie's Secret Formula. It was a good thing. That year, our class decided to celebrate the ending of the school year with a swimming party. I was horrified. How would I cover my legs, arms, and chest with a one-piece swimming suit? I had tried before. It didn't work. In fact, I couldn't even keep a Speedo in its rightful spot—without suspenders.

The very week of their announcement, The Secret Formula arrived.

I eagerly tore open the package. *Time is short,* I thought, *this had better be instant.* Inside were drawings of an extremely muscular man doing exercises. That was it. No drink. No clever little formula. Just a workout list accompanied by illustrations of some guy who had muscles in places I didn't even have places. Undaunted, I descended to our basement and began the Charles Atlas Gaunt to Gargantuan Health and Nutrition Plan.

During the next few months those instructions were followed religiously: I did push-ups with my feet on a chair. I did sit-ups with my legs in the air. I did chin-ups, leg-lifts, wrist-rolls, knee-jerks. You name 'em, I did 'em. A thousand times over.

The night before school was dismissed, the class—in its infinite wisdom—cancelled the swimming party.

Throughout my high school years, however, I continued the program. I was determined that if ever they announced another swimming party, I could recline unashamedly on a beach towel. Even if they had to carry me there—in a pine box. You know what? The formula didn't work. Oh, I suppose I learned a few things about discipline, but I must tell you, I'm almost as skinny today as the day I opened that package. In fact, I still can't force the scales past 163 without carry-on luggage.

The funny thing is, I really don't mind. The turning point came the day I discovered that Charles Atlas didn't have The Secret Formula after all. An ancient king by the name of David did. I was reading the book of Psalms when his words hit me:

> For you created my inmost being; you knit me together in my mother's womb. I praise you because I am fearfully and wonderfully made; your works are wonderful, I know that full well. My frame was not hidden from you when I was made in the secret place. When I was woven together in the depths of the earth, your eyes saw my unformed body. All the days ordained for me were written in your book before one of them came to be (Psalm 139:13-16).

I read it again. And again. Then I memorized it. And today when I gaze into a full-length mirror, I remember those verses and I smile from ear to ear. Not because I'm able to chase anyone from the beach. Or because I'm overwhelmed by my attractiveness. But because the One who spoke the stars into space called my name. Because the One who crafted the mountains and hollowed out the ocean depths left His fingerprints all over me. Because God Himself would rather die than live without me.

Tonight, I think we'll celebrate. I think we'll pile the kids into the car and go out for ice cream. And then we'll go swimming. I'll try to remember to throw in some suspenders.

11

The Most Amazing Story of All

WHEN YOU ARE BORN and raised in the buckle of the Bible belt, and the worst sin you have committed is pulling your sister's pigtails or feeding gum to the neighbor's cat, you envy people like Lester Schwartz. Mr. Schwartz blew through our Christian school most Septembers with the most amazing personal testimony I had ever heard. He was a former felon with real tattoos, and Lester's life had been marred by things we did not talk about at our dinner table. Things like drugs and drinking and murder. When Mr. Schwartz came to school, we children listened wide-eared from the edges of our chapel pews as his delightfully awful story unfolded, and when he reached the part about his escape from prison in a hot air balloon, we couldn't help ourselves. We broke into spontaneous applause. As I recall, it was probably the loudest response I had heard since the missionary from Africa held up a Black Mamba snake skin which a cluster of second-grade girls thought to be alive.

During the following weeks we reenacted certain parts of Lester's story in schoolyard games, and the following September the excitement increased with the nearness of Mr. Schwartz's return. Finally, the day arrived. "We have a special guest this morning," said the school secretary, Miss Hale, who stood no taller than she sat. "Some of you may remember him from last year, but let's give him a warm Alberta welcome just the same." The older kids whispered to the younger ones, and both groups clapped eagerly. Mr. Schwartz stood, dwarfing Miss Hale, who sat down and pulled out a hanky.

"You may have heard mah story before," he began, rolling up his sleeves, "but I think it bears repeatin'. I don't tell you this 'cuz I'm proud of it, yuh understand, I just hope I can save some of you little 'uns the troubles I been through."

As I listened to his story for the second time, a curious feeling came over me. It was envy, pure and simple. I would kill to have lived such a life. But my story wasn't worth telling. At the tender age of five, my mother and I knelt by my Styrofoam bed one night as I asked Jesus to come into my heart and forgive me for things like raiding Mrs. Pike's forbidden raspberries and not liking Sundays. *Who wants to hear a story like that?* I asked myself. And so, as the others listened to Lester, I invented a new one. It was the best testimony a ten-year-old could think of, and two weeks later I arrived at our Friday Sing and Share chapel, ready to deliver.

We had just finished singing "It only takes a spark to get a fire going" when Miss Hale stood to her feet. Or at least I think she was standing. "Does anyone have something to share?" she asked. I waited an agonizing two or three seconds, then rose to my feet, carefully rehearsing what I planned to say.

"I'm not proud of this," I would say, folding my hands and looking my schoolmates in the eyes, "but this summer I made a hundred thousand bucks dealing drugs." Gasps would surround me. Miss Hale would haul out the hanky. Maybe faint. But I would continue undaunted: "Oh, I know it sounds like a lot to swallow coming from a kid who's only ten years old and lives just up the hill, but I guess I fell in with the wrong crowd.

"It all started the day Juan Gomez drove slowly by our house, eyeing the shed where we kept our rabbits, Fudge and Marshmallow. Juan was tall for a Colombian, and underneath his sunglasses his eyes were red and tired. He stopped his black Cadillac, slid the window down and motioned me over from the swing set. 'Hey,' he said, holding up a wad of twenties, 'you wanna buy lots of gum?'

"The temptation was too great for me, and before I knew it I was sneaking out at night to fly with Juan by Lear jet between Colombia and our baseball field. We stashed the drugs in our shed along with huge piles of money, and I was back in bed before the sun was up. It was a great life for about a week, but I started getting tired of all that gum and candy. One day, Fudge and Marshmallow started acting real weird. Dad said it looked like they were from another planet or something, not human rabbits at all. The next morning, I was reading in my personal devotions where it says that all of us have sinned and, well, I asked God's forgiveness right then and there, and I knew I'd have to do something about the shed. So that night I let the rabbits go and stuffed the shed with sticks of dynamite that I'd bought at Vaughn's Hardware earlier that day. Then I lit a long fuse and climbed into bed. Some of you may remember the bang."

At this point, Miss Hale would probably blow her nose and I would have to wait while she regained some composure. Then I would continue. "Juan came by the next day looking for the shed. But all he could find were two rabbits running in funny circles on some charcoal, and my daddy and me arm in arm, surveying the damage. That was the last I saw of Juan. He didn't stick around to find out what happened. But my father knew everything. I told him. And when I did, he hugged me and said that I had learned some valuable lessons: that I should choose my friends carefully and that money will eventually go up in smoke. Then we knelt on the charcoal and prayed."

The story had come together quite nicely in my mind, and I was thinking that an altar call would be a real possibility, when suddenly I realized that my sister Ruth had come to chapel that day. The sister I had pinched. The one who knew about my summer, who knew it wasn't like that.

"Did you have something to say, Philip?" asked Miss Hale.

"Who, me? Uh . . . I . . . um . . . just wanted to say that I had a really good summer."

"Why, thank you," she said. And I sat down.

❊❊❊

Three or four years passed before I worked up the courage to confess my imaginings to my father. When I did, he smiled a lot, then said some things I've mostly forgotten. But I got the impression talking to Dad that day that sometimes little boys whose worst crimes are committed in raspberry patches are the toughest criminals of all. I didn't know what he meant, but I'm starting to understand. You see, it's easy to go through life looking at the gaping wounds of those around us. We'll find plenty of them these days. But too often those who focus on the sins of others miss their own. "Every one of us is a sinner," Dad said, "No matter how dull or exciting our testimony." The Bible says it best: "For it is by grace you have been saved, through faith—and this not from yourselves, it is the gift of God—not by works, so that no one can boast" (Ephesians 2:8,9).

When we kneel before God one day and hear His "Welcome Home," some will celebrate the pit He brought them out of, and some the pit He kept them from, but all of us will celebrate God's grace. Nothing more. Nothing less. Nothing else.

The more I think about it, the more I realize it's the most amazing story of them all.

CHAPTER

12

Broken Records

ONE OF THE FIRST things that attracted me to my wife was the way she smashed things in the kitchen. When we were first going out (to this day I'm not sure where we were going, but that's not the point), I remember standing outside the front door with my index finger poised an inch from the doorbell. Then I heard it: "Whoops!" followed a split second later by a distinctly familiar crashing sound. A sound that reminded me of home. *Ah,* I thought, *this is the woman for me. She is just like my mother.* When I was a kid I spent a lot of time on the kitchen floor. Sometimes people ask me where I got my sense of humor. I say, "I spent a lot of time going around in circles on the kitchen floor. I'm dizzy, okay?"

You had to be careful on that floor. My mother was not always content to break one dish. She would break entire sets. *Whoops!* She broke other items, too. Once she broke a spanking spoon on my rear end. Okay, I'd better be honest. This happened more than once. And when I got a little older she used to break vinyl records over her knee. *Snap!* A perfectly good Beatles record. Probably worth thousands today. But there was one thing she never seemed to break: her word. If Mom said she would do something, she did it. Her words were commandments, etched in stone, but not always heeded. "You talk like that again, son, and I'll wash your mouth out with soap." I can't recall the word or why I deemed its usage necessary, but thirty years later I can still taste the soap. New and Improved Dove. If I'm outside when the memory comes along, I look around me, then I spit twice.

Mom did not limit herself to soap, however. She kept the cupboard stocked high with Cayenne pepper. "You sing that again and you'll burn for it," she told my brother Tim, who had taken to revising some of her favorite hymns and teaching them to his impressionable little brother:

> My hope is built on nothing less
> Than Scofield's notes and Scripture Press.
> I dare not trust the Word alone
> 'Cuz I can't read it on my own.

I had no idea what a Scofield was, nor a Cayenne for that matter, but I was destined to taste one of them. As Tim stood defiantly on the sofa, I joined him in the glad refrain:

> On top of Old Smokey all covered with sand,
> I shot my poor teacher with a red rubber band.
> I shot her with pleasure, I shot her with pride.
> How could I miss her? She's thirty feet wide.

(Actually, we sang another version of this song. One which I cannot print and am still trying to forget.)

To this day I despise Cayenne pepper. You put it in a casserole and I can smell it driving by your house eating chocolate ice cream at 60 miles an hour with my windows rolled up. Mom seemed to like it, though. She piled it high on spoon handles, then inched it slowly in the direction of our tightly sealed mouths. Tim usually felt a need to clear his sinuses at this point, *humfff,* and the dreaded pepper would cascade to the floor in glorious rainbows of red. We thought this was so funny, we doubled over with laughter. Until Mom stacked the hot stuff higher.

I took up running that day. A kid can only handle so much, you know, so I took off across a field, wondering what would happen if I just kept going and wasn't heard from again. "Kid missing, police follow hot trail," would make a good headline.

OFFICER ONE: "Frank, I think I may have something here."

OFFICER TWO: "What is it, Biff?"

OFFICER ONE (sniffing his hand): "It's a trail of tiny red particles . . . smells like some sorta pepper."

Instead of being a statistic, however, I chose to be a tattletale. Showing up at a friend's house, I squealed on my mom. "She WHAT?" he said, amazement crossing his eyes.

"Ya, and it was hotter than the dickens."

"My momma wouldn't do that," he said, slowly shaking his head. "What's a dicken?"

Upon my arrival home later that afternoon, Mom told me most emphatically not to leave the yard again without asking permission. "Or," she said, "I will . . . um . . . I will

. . . put you on the dog leash and tie you to the clothes-line." *No way,* I thought. *She wouldn't.* But she did. The next day I ignored her warning and ran away once again. When I returned, Mom was waiting, like Charlton Heston, stone tablets in hand. And this is true: She placed Inky's red collar about my neck, clipped it to the leash, and swung me out to dry.

When I told this to my seven-year-old recently, he asked with wide eyes, "Were your feet touching the ground?"

"Yes, but barely," I replied. "It's why I'm so tall." Actually, I told him the truth: She didn't swing me out to dry, but I sat on our back step, thoroughly enjoying myself. I'd never seen the world quite this way before.

Like turtles, neighbor ladies poked their heads out windows. "That Bernice Callaway has gone too far this time," they said, shaking their necks. "She's gone clean over the edge."

"Hey," I shot back, sitting up straight. "I ran away, okay? I disobeyed. I'm getting what I deserve." They weren't so sure.

When I remind Mom of the incident, she winces a little. And when I tell others of my being collared, I get mixed reactions. Most laugh. But some sound like the turtles in our neighborhood. "The child was abused," they say behind their hands. "One of these days he'll just up and start barking uncontrollably."

But there is one reason they are wrong. There is one reason I don't have to battle past scars to tell of my childhood. It is simply this: The same hands that spanked me, held me. The same voice that spoke doom and gloom, often whispered "I love you." And I never once doubted that the whisper was true. After all, when love is remembered, much is forgotten. My mother may have broken some rules, but she loved me. My mother may have broken some things, but she kept her word.

Broken dishes. Broken records. Broken spanking spoons. Makes me think of something I broke just a few short years ago. It's a little embarrassing, but if you promise not to tell, I'll let you in on a humiliating little secret in the next chapter.

13

About Lawn Order

I READ RECENTLY of a man in Wyoming who attended a farm auction completely unaware that he was about to hit the jackpot. The auction started the way all auctions start, with the junk being bought up first. Buckets of bolts and wires and nuts and knobs were going for about three bucks apiece, so the man bought six of them and lugged them home to a wife who said, "Don't bring that junk in here," but changed her tune rather quickly when her dear husband uncovered beneath some tired rubber bands an 1856 jade-colored half penny worth seventy-five hundred dollars. "Not bad work for a Saturday," he later told the media, then went out and bought his wife a winter coat.

I got to thinking about that coat Saturday morning when my dad awoke me and offered to buy me a breakfast of bacon and eggs if I would accompany him to an auction. It was the offer of bacon and eggs that attracted me most, I must admit. I have attended just two auctions in my life, and I'm sure the amount of cigarette smoke I inhaled has sucked five years out of my life. "Even people who don't smoke, smoke at these things," said my father. "They're scared someone else will claim their prize."

Dad wasn't smoking but he was sweating a little as the bidding started on his prize—an electric lawnmower he'd been eyeing since our arrival. "Mint condition," he whispered. "That's what the widow said." The bidding started at five dollars, and by the time it hit thirty-five, Dad was chewing his nails. At forty-five, there was a welcome silence, and when the auctioneer reached fifty, Dad nodded nonchalantly as if he didn't really care either way. "Going once, going twice, gone . . ."

"Let's put her in the trunk and head for home," said Dad, whose nervous energy had turned to excitement. "It can't get better than this."

On the way home I reminded him that he already had a lawnmower, and he said, "I know. I bought it for you." It was a Christmas present in June, he said, something that would keep me from driving across town to borrow his.

⁂

I tuned that lawnmower up the very week a new neighbor moved in next door. When I went to introduce myself he said, "Hi, I'm Vance. May I borrow your toolbox?" So began a meaningful friendship that has grown with the passing of time—and of food, tapes, catalogs, books, even articles of clothing. Yes, within one month of moving in, Vance had borrowed almost everything I owned except my electric lawnmower. "Electric lawnmowers are for wimps," he told me. "Mine's a gas-powered lawnmower. A *man's* lawnmower. It'll trim anything."

I didn't appreciate the way he italicized *man's* but I had to admit that he was right. My fifty-dollar Christmas present was never, even in its prime, very healthy. By July it was growing sicker and sicker each time I plugged it in, and by September people were coming from other time zones to see what the noise was. I was pulling in higher ratings than Major League Baseball.

RUSSIAN HUSBAND: "Wow, Honey! Did you hear that?"

RUSSIAN WIFE: "I think it's coming from Chernobyl."

Yes, with one flip of a switch I could cause a power surge that would turn lights off all over town. So, without telling my poor father, I relegated it to a garage sale and attached a sign:

USED LAWNMOWER. NEEDS WORK. MECHANIC'S DREAM.

Then I humbled myself, went next door, and borrowed Vance's.

He grinned widely as he demonstrated the pull-start mechanism. "Be careful with her," he said. "She sorta wants to jump out of the starting blocks all on her own."

Vance was right. That day I cut the grass in record time and slid the lawnmower into its rightful spot by lunchtime. A week later I humbled myself again. But this time Vance was gone. *No problem,* I thought. *We are close friends now. I will borrow it and top up the gas tank when I'm done.*

After clearing my yard of enough trucks, dolls, wagons, and balls to open a competitive toy store chain, I firmly inserted my fluorescent orange ear plugs and gave the lawnmower two swift pulls.

It started.

Looking back now, I see that I should have shut it off right then. I should have removed the ear plugs and pushed the mower back to Vance's shed. Instead I proceeded to trim our backyard.

It was smooth cutting. Until I reached The Stump— six inches of pine sticking two inches out of the ground. A lawnmower this powerful should clear The Stump with no problem, I reasoned, the ear plugs clearly blocking the flow of anything at all to my brain area. Besides, anything sticking this far out of the ground could be hazardous to your children and should be trimmed.

BAAAANG.

Then nothing. I tried the pull-start mechanism. It would not pull. I turned the lawnmower over and gazed at the carnage. Now, please understand that I am not a mechanical person. I know that the engine in most cars is somewhere near the front, that's about it. But when I saw oil flowing freely onto the blades and the thingee holding the blades bent at a 45-degree angle, I decided to do what my father had faithfully drummed into me so many years ago: "Philip," he had said, "when you borrow something, always return it."

I pushed the lawnmower next door and slid it into that rightful spot. *Vance has mechanical abilities,* I thought to myself. *He will be able to borrow my tools and fix it.*

Then I went across the street to my neighbor Jim's house. Jim is known on our block for a pretty fair lawnmower but, more than that, his ability to keep a secret.

"You won't believe this," I told him. "I hit a stump."

"No kidding," he replied, rolling his eyes. "They heard it in Cairo."

"Uh, do you mind if I borrow *your* lawnmower?"

"Sure," he replied, "Or shall we just get a sledgehammer and smash it right here in *my* yard?"

"Was that a no?"

"Yes," he said. "Besides, I think I've misplaced it."

Later that day I left town on a five-day business trip.

Upon my return, Vance was waiting in my driveway.

"Hi, my friend," I said, "I brought you a Snickers bar from Washington, D.C."

He got right to the point. "Do you mind if I borrow your flashlight?"

Whew, all is well, I thought. *All is normal.* "Sure thing, I'll get it."

And I did. But when I handed him the flashlight, Vance motioned, "Come with me," and I knew I was in trouble.

Now you must understand that Vance is bigger than I. In fact, comparatively speaking, one of us plays rugby, the other rides racehorses. We had just begun the slow walk out to my backyard when Vance turned and began to club me on the head with the flashlight. Slowly I sank to my knees in the darkness. Not really. But I sincerely wondered if he would. Instead, Vance led me out to The Stump. And, I kid you not: Surrounding The Stump was a "POLICE LINE DO NOT CROSS" yellow ribbon. Vance had poured ketchup over The Stump, and on the ground he had sprayed the white outline of a lawnmower.

"We have a suspect," smiled Vance.

"What do you mean *we?*"

"Jim and I."

Jim walked rather sheepishly out from behind a tree. "Hi!" he said.

Then the two of them took me to the garden where all that protruded from a small mound of earth was the handle-bar of a stainless steel lawnmower. A large gray brick marked the spot. Etched upon the brick was this eulogy:

Here lies Mr. Mower
★★★

A life so quickly taken
by a hand so quick to take.
He will never mow
what life had
in the grass ahead of him.

I don't know what your friends are like. But, believe it or not, I sincerely wish for you friends like mine. Friends like James, Kevin, and Harold—even Jim and Vance. Friends I can laugh with. Friends who are too smart to look for perfection when choosing companions. Friends who care enough to face me with the truth about myself. And, yes, friends who are willing and able . . . to forgive.

Well, it's time to close this chapter. Besides, I really better go. The phone is ringing. It could be Dad asking me to go to tomorrow's auction. Or it may be Vance looking for the next payment on his new lawnmower.

14

St. Ida and the Green Cotton Pants

MISS IDA WEISMULLER was my fifth-grade teacher and to this day I believe God has a very special place for her in heaven. I also believe that St. Peter will salute her respectfully when she arrives, and that he will hand her the keys to a glorious mansion right next door to that of Job, who suffered great physical and mental travail while on this earth. They will have much to talk about. The mansion will undoubtedly be located far from any school districts or playgrounds, in a quiet section of heaven where there is not too much rejoicing for the first few thousand years.

Miss Weismuller began her teaching career in our fifth-grade classroom, a classroom with west windows and wooden chairs populated by ten-year-old boys who collectively had the IQ of a birch-bark canoe.

To complicate matters, Miss Weismuller was a recent immigrant from Germany and spoke English sometimes. An English she punctuated with heavy exclamation marks. She was a tall woman, Miss Weismuller. Her clothing had been purchased during bleaker times, and she always had a bun in her hair that was drawn too tight to allow her much smiling. She had no children of her own, no nieces, no nephews, a fact that was painfully evident the day she asked me to come to the front to receive my punishment for making the other children laugh. "Philip!" she ordered, "You vill shtand here, *ja!* And face za class! Now!" And I did. While she taught mathematics I stood beside her obediently, quietly facing my fellow classmates, as I was commanded.

Now, please understand that I was a good-natured child, not necessarily looking for trouble, but if it presented itself, if it hit me over the head and said, "Hey, here I am! What you gonna do with me?" I was usually gracious enough to take it by the hand. As I stood before the class that day, I thought to myself: *This is not punishment. Not for a comedian. Putting my earlobes in Vise-Grips is punishment. This is the knock of opportunity.*

And so, as she turned away to etch fractions on the blackboard, I, with straight face, wiggled my left hand from my pants pocket, eased it between my shirt buttons and placed it snugly under my right armpit. Lifting my arm and crossing my eyes, I brought the arm down slowly. And brought the house down too. The entire classroom erupted in glorious laughter and a smattering of applause.

I don't know if you have ever been hit on the body by flying chalk or felt the dull thud of a blackboard eraser between your shoulder blades, but it paled in comparison to the pain I felt trying to walk from the office half an hour later. "Bend over, Philip!" said Miss Weismuller, in pretty good English. "And touch yer toes, *javol!*"

From that day onward I occupied a special place in her gaze, right at the front of the classroom, right under her glasses. I wish I could tell you that I straightened up thereafter. That I sat with folded hands, admiring her hairdo and learning about fractions. But lying has never taken me far. By February, Saint Ida had asked me to touch my toes several more times, and by early spring I was earning quite a reputation among the music faculty as well. One day I brought a safety pin to class for research purposes and discovered that I could cause fellow students to rise again. And again. It was not the first time our instructor had taken notice of me, but this time she threw up her baton and sent me back to see Miss Weismuller.

I was frightened as I stood before her that day. She towered above me like a cat just waiting to pounce.

"And vhat," she asked in a voice that would have sent Napoleon scurrying from Italy, "is ze punishment for being kicked out of music class three times in a row, Philip?" My name she tossed out much like one would a month-old tuna casserole.

Unable to force the word through my quivering lips, I picked up a pencil and wrote "strap" in very small letters. It was while handing the paper to her that I realized I was closing in on some kind of record. In one year the rod of correction had graced my seat of understanding more times than all my siblings put together.

If you were ever strapped in school yourself, you know that there were certain positive aspects to the whole experience. For one thing, you were a celebrity for up to 24 hours. Classmates would line the halls to ask what it felt like.

"Did you cry?" they asked.

"Did it hurt?"

"Naw," I lied.

For some reason no one ever asked, "Well then, while you were in there did you happen to see who was doing all that screaming?"

Instead they would ask, "What did you get it for?"

"I put a pin in Stan Kirk," I said, trying to hide my pride.

"Wow," they said, and I strutted down the hall, leaving them standing in small circles of respectful conversation.

I was unable to ride my bike home later that day. But as I walked home with Steve Porr, I told him my thoughts: "I think it's my pants," I said.

He stopped throwing dirt clods and looked at me. "The pants?"

"Ya. Every time I get sent to the office I look down and I have these same green pants on."

"She doesn't like your pants?"

"No, I don't think that's it."

"Well, where did you get them?" he asked, looking at my pants.

"That's not the point," I said. "The point is we've got to do something about these pants."

"Like what? Burn 'em?"

"That's the most ridiculous idea I've heard this week," I said, "so let's do it!"

And so it was that we found ourselves basking in the warm glow of a bonfire that June afternoon. Yes—believe it or not—we burned my green cotton pants in our brick backyard fireplace.

"Do you suppose a little demon might run out?" Steve asked, ever eager to discuss the supernatural.

"I don't know. Let's watch." And we did. But we saw nothing unusual. Neighbors did. But not us.

That was 25 years ago, and I must admit that I'm just as scared today as the day I stood before Miss Weismuller and wrote "strap" on a small slip of paper.

You see, I have school-age children of my own.

And September's coming.

I also know "by heart" a lot of Scripture verses including the one about the sins of the fathers visiting the children. So as I weigh these thoughts, I find myself asking the same question that Galileo and like-minded individuals undoubtedly pondered throughout written history: "Is there any hope at all for my offspring?"

The obvious answer is "no." Anyone who superstitiously burned his pants in grade five is bound to have serious problems raising kids. And I find little comfort in the words of those who would prescribe *only* the latest child-rearing techniques.

The answer, I believe, is found in the lives of parents like mine, who preached the gospel all the time and occasionally used words. Almost every morning I came down the hall hoping something was cooking and there was Mom, kneeling by her rocking chair, praying for me. "Oh God," I heard her say once, "do something with Philip." Mom and Dad talked about me more on their knees than anywhere else. If it weren't for those prayers, I'm convinced that I'd be walking the same wide path that too many of my friends are. We all must choose. And so I'll be praying every day that the same God who loved a mischievous little troublemaker enough to turn his life around will do as much for his children.

My wife is in full agreement. She just returned from a shopping spree and has managed to snag a great little outfit for Stephen's first day of school. It's a white pullover with the number 32 on the front, and—would you believe it?—a pair of green cotton pants.

There's another reason for hope. It's the best one of all. Miss Weismuller will help me tell you about it in the next chapter.

15

My Tombstone

IF I HAD TO PICK my favorite year in school, I'd take grade five in a minute. In fact, I spent four very fine years there (just kidding).

This was the year Miss Weismuller came to town to conduct experiments in our classroom. I was one of those experiments. In September, she assigned me a spot behind Bobby Spaulding (a brilliant and discerning young man who laughed at all of my jokes) and across the aisle from a weepy girl with horn-rimmed spectacles and a name I can't recall. I was moved around the classroom after that, like a wandering Gypsy, without home or country, and by January I had developed a fond dislike for the strap. I suppose I did not care for Miss Weismuller, either. She was too strict—I felt—and her lips were puckered, as if she spent her evenings sucking buttons off a sofa. I pointed these things out to my mother one evening and received a clear message: "She's your teacher, Philip. You may not like her, but you will show her respect. She has been put there for a purpose and . . . um . . . I'm sure we will one day know what that purpose is." I wasn't quite sure what Mom meant, but I knew her sentiments were not shared by all the parents.

In mid-March, one mother stormed angrily past the principal of our Christian school, past Miss Weismuller and into our classroom. There she removed her son—books, pencils, eraser, and all. He never returned. Moved clean out of the district, some said. We students watched with interest as the dust settled and, strangely, found ourselves siding with Miss Weismuller. For the next 15 minutes we listened to her every word, refrained from joke-telling, and kept quiet without being told. But such things come to an end, and for me the ending was high in drama.

"Put your books away, *ja,*" said Miss Weismuller, as the clock wound down to 3 P.M. "It is time for our Bible memory test." The words struck horror into my ten-year-old heart. Once a month we wrote out verses from the Bible, and our marks were clearly reflected in our report cards. My marks had been slipping ever since kindergarten, and this month they were destined to slip even further. I had been too busy with lesser things to store away Scripture. And so, I slid some verse cards from my desk, lodged them on the chair between my legs, smiled saintlike at the weepy girl across the aisle, and in desperation, began to cheat on my Bible verses.

Believe it or not, this is what I wrote: "My little children, these things write I unto you that ye sin not."

I stopped, looked at the blackboard, and hoped I hadn't been writing too fast.

The verse continued: "And if any man sin we have an advocate with the Father, Jesus Christ the righteous: And he is the propitiation for our sins: and not for ours only, but also for the sins of the whole world."

The other children were writing dutifully. A few were scratching their heads and furrowing their brows. I continued: "And hereby we do know that we know him, if we keep his commandments. He that saith, I know him, and keepeth not his commandments, is a liar, and the truth is not in him. But whoso keepeth his word, in him verily is the love of God perfected." I even wrote out the reference correctly: "1 John 2:1-5."

Sleep was slow in coming that night. Oh, my report card would be looking better, but in the darkness tidy report cards don't hold a candle to clean consciences. *You are a liar, Phil, and the truth is not in you.* Quietly I made my way into my parents' bedroom and tapped my mother on the shoulder.

She sat up straight. "Palestine!" she said, then breathed deeply and asked, "What's wrong?"

"Nothin'," I replied.

"Son, it's almost midnight . . . what's the matter?"

"Mom," I said in muffled tones, "I cheeddonahuhm."

"You what?"

"Ah Mom, I cheated on my memory verses."

She got out of bed and knelt beside me. We talked and then we prayed, asking God's forgiveness. I was leaving the room feeling a whole lot lighter—when Mom stopped me in my tracks: "You will have to tell Miss Weismuller, too."

About an hour later I drifted fitfully in and out of a dream that haunts me to this day:

The punishment is administered in the schoolyard, in the heat of afternoon recess. The children are lined up alphabetically, according to height. Ministers from the surrounding area gather, wearing black suits and solemn expressions. The mayor is there. He introduces Miss Ida Weismuller's speech, and all the schoolchildren listen attentively. "We are gathered here today to witness the conclusion of an awful blight on each one of our reputations, *javol!*" The younger children strain their necks to get a good look at me. The older ones simply nod their agreement and look away. Bobby Spaulding isn't laughing. Miss Weismuller isn't finished: "Today I have learned that Philip Ronald Callaway cheated on his Bible memory verses." A collective gasp arises. The girl from across the aisle removes her horn-rimmed spectacles and dabs the corners of her eyes. Miss Weismuller continues with little emotion: "Let each of us resolve to conduct ourselves in an obedient and orderly fashion, with sobriety and prudence, lest we end up like this poor young man. This . . . this . . . *cheater.*"

The children file past me in a solemn procession, from the youngest to the oldest. Each is handed a stick, which they toss with a sigh into a pile around the swingset leg to which I am tied. The ministers strike matches and toss them on the sticks. Emotionless, Miss Weismuller fans the flames. With my report card.

No, I did not sleep well that night.

The small graveside service held the following Tuesday is attended by my parents only. My sister and brothers are too ashamed to come. They study algebra instead. *He cheated on his Bible memory,* they remind each other in hushed tones. But in later years they sneak into the graveyard late at night, their flashlights searching out my tiny tombstone and the words:

THE UNKNOWN STUDENT
1961–1971

For habits he would not break
He was ceremoniously burned at the stake
His sins are too many to list
He certainly will not be missed.

May we *rest in peace.*

The next morning I crept bleary-eyed into the school building. Early. The other students weren't there yet, but Miss Weismuller was. She waited inside the courtroom, gavel in hand. I tapped on the door. "Come in," said a thick accent. I opened the door obediently. She sat behind her desk, dressed mostly in black. My judge. My jury. My executioner.

"Vhat is it?"

I forced myself forward and stood still before her. "I came to tell you that . . . I'm sorry," I said, unable to look up. "I . . . um . . . cheated on Bible memory yesterday."

"And how did you cheat, Philip?"

"I copied off the verse cards."

"Did anyone see you?"

"I don't think so."

"Did *God* see you?"

I looked up for the first time. "Yes," I said. "He kept me awake last night."

Tiny traces of a smile formed around her eyes. "Then you've asked His forgiveness, *ja?*"

"Yes."

She smiled widely in spite of the bun in her hair. "Then I forgive you, too," she said. "After school today you will take the test over, but I forgive you."

From that day on, I didn't cheat on another test. Oh, I was accused of it once in high school. I got 73 on a math test, and my teacher said, "No way." But I didn't do it. And I think I know why. You see, way back in fifth grade a teacher who had every reason to pronounce judgment smiled. And offered me grace.

You are a liar, and the truth is not in you.
Yes. But God forgave me.
You cheated on Bible memory.
Yes. But I told Miss Weismuller. And she forgave me, too.

Thanks to that forgiveness I won't have the previous epitaph etched on my headstone. I've had a lot of years to think about it, and this is what I'd like my tombstone to say:

He found God's grace
too amazing
to keep to himself.

It seems Miss Weismuller taught me more than either of us expected.

If I had to pick my favorite year in school, I'd pick grade five in a minute.

Parenting 101

Years ago a pastor conducted a popular seminar titled "Thirteen Surefire Rules for Raising Children." Then he had some kids of his own. And changed the seminar to: "Six Suggestions for Raising Children." When his kids became teenagers, he became a plumber. I think it was Bill Cosby who said, "You know the only people who are always sure about the proper way to raise children? Those who never had any." But you know something? Parents who live on their knees discover that God will provide us with all that we need: love, wisdom, discernment, and Extra-Strength Tylenol. And they just may encounter another key ingredient to parenting: a good sense of humor. Parents need to unwrap the gift of laughter often. As you are about to see.

16

The Day My Angel Lost Her Halo

"Jesus love me, dis I doe. For the Bible tell me so . . ."

The sound filters my way from across the hall. It is six in the morning. Saturday morning. Putting a pillow over my head, I manage to smile and drift off again.

"Jesus love me, dis I doe. For the Bible tell me so . . ." The record is stuck, and the volume is up. I put another pillow over my head.

"LITTLE ONES TO HIM BEE-ONG. THEY ARE WEAK, BUT HE IS STRONG!" I am out of pillows. And patience. Sitting up, I grope for my ear plugs. They are nowhere to be felt. Beside me lies my wife. Bone of my bone, flesh of my flesh. She appears to be in a deep sleep. I'm not so sure.

The song starts again. Propping the pillows up, I lean back and listen.

It seems like only yesterday that the singer was born. It was a frightening day for me. I was prepared for the process,

I had been through it once before, but I was unprepared for the result: the cutest little girl since, well, since my wife. So why was I frightened? Well, I knew all about little boys. I had been one. I had had one. Boys played football. And wrestled. And spit. Boys slammed doors and made big messes in small bathrooms. But little girls? I hadn't a clue what they did. I had seen them pushing dolls along tree-lined streets, and helping their mothers hang out the wash, so this much I knew: Little girls were direct descendants of angels. The last two years have confirmed my theory. Oh sure, there were times when Rachael's halo had been slightly askew, like the time she hung porridge from her little brother. But a sinner she was not. Theologians may differ with me there, but I had irrefutable evidence. I had a daughter.

There, see? This girl of angelic ancestry has stopped singing and fallen asleep. I think I will, too.

✥✥✥

"Hey Rachael, we do not pour milk on the floor." It is brunch time and all is not well. My angel-daughter is staring at me, and for the first time since her birth day she has defiance in her eyes. Looking directly at me, she continues to drain the cup.

"Rachael, you stop it right now."

"No," she says, her halo slipping rapidly.

"Will you obey Daddy?"

"No," she says.

I repeat the question. She repeats her answer: "No."

What to do? Gently removing her from the chair, I carry her down the hall to the bedroom.

Now, at this point, several people are having conversations in my head.

GRANDMA: "What that girl needs is a little more love."

SOCIAL WORKER: "Whatever you do, don't spank her. Spanking is bad modeling. It teaches a child to hit others."

GRANDPA: "Since when did you have to teach a child to hit? They come out of the womb swinging. I say you spank the tar out of her."

SOCIAL WORKER: "I have evidence that spanking leads to a poor self-image. Your child may develop a negative opinion of herself—the idea that she is bad."

GRANDPA: "Well, she hasn't exactly been good."

SOCIAL WORKER: "But spanking encourages children to avoid getting caught."

PSYCHOLOGIST: "She just needs a time out. Let her sit over there by herself and think about her bad decision."

GRANDPA: "Oh, give me a break."

GRANDMA: "I say we spank the social worker . . ."

"Rachael, will you obey Daddy?" I ask, thinking that perhaps she misunderstood the question.

"No," she says, looking me straight in the eyes as if to say, "Didn't you ask that before?"

I hold her on my lap and talk with her. Then I repeat my question. Her answer has not changed. In the hallway her older brother is on a "just say 'yes'" campaign, but his sister remains woefully defiant. I hold her, I cry with her, I pray for wisdom, and then—I spank her.

Still she says no.

I am a basket case by now. "Dear God," I pray out loud, "help my little girl, help her to obey." Then the tears come down my face and they won't stop. One falls on Rachael's sleeve. She looks up at me and sniffles, "Yes, obey." Fifteen minutes later she is asleep in my arms.

⚘⚘⚘

It is nearing midnight now. I've been out playing hockey with the guys. Weary and sweating, I stand outside Rachael's room. Soft breathing tells me she's asleep. Lego blocks are scattered on the covers, and in one corner Cuddle Bear rests on his head.

I kneel beside her bed, stroke her blonde hair, and shake my head. What a difference a few hours can make. "The Lord bless you and keep you, Rachael," I pray. "The Lord make His face to shine upon you and be gracious unto you. The Lord turn His face toward you and give you peace. Amen."

Opening her eyes, she looks up at me. "Come," I say. She grins and reaches up.

We sit together on the couch. "I can't sleep after I play hockey, Rachael. Maybe you'll be an incurable insomniac, too." The words hold little meaning for her, but the voice does. She's followed me around the house since she said "yes." She's told me she "lubs" me a dozen times, and just as often she's wanted me to pick her up and hold her. Now she presses closer. As I hug her tight, I commit myself again to one of the most important of human relationships: that of a father and his daughter.

"Lord," I pray out loud, "give me wisdom and courage to bring this child up in the way she should go. Help me be consistent in discipline and liberal in healthy affection."

I would like to say that my prayer put her to sleep. But after I tucked her in, she could be heard humming. And in the morning, her halo was firmly in place. Daddy's little angel was singing her favorite song. After all, it was time to get up. It was six o'clock.

17

Kids in the Kingdom

For much of my life my priorities were somewhat suspect. For instance, golf followed baseball which followed hockey which followed . . . well, I can't think of anything it followed. Like many Canadian boys, I ate and slept sports. In November, my brothers and I would lace up our ice skates and leave them on until Mother pried them off sometime in late March. Long summer days were spent chasing anything that could be kicked, rolled, slid, or bounced. Evenings we conducted "phone-in sports talk shows" and entertained dreams of future stardom.

Of course, having children of our own has a way of helping us rearrange those priorities. And it started for me in the most unlikely of places: the golf course.

Tightly gripping my trusty 3-wood, I addressed the ball. Before me lay the neatly groomed greenery of the first hole. Behind me stood my son. This summer I have bought a membership, sawed off a 7-iron, in hopes of teaching my son everything there is to know about this game I have come to love. Since golf is better caught than taught, I would demonstrate. He, I hoped, would catch. I was confident. Poised. Certain.

"Watch, Stephen," I said.

Firmly planting my feet, I brought the club back and in one smooth, practiced motion sliced a brand new Top Flite into the muddiest creek this side of the Amazon. I was not a happy golfer.

"Did it go in the water?"

"Yes, Stephen."

"Is that how you do it?"

"Uh . . . well, not exactly. Let me try again."

Several holes and a dozen balls later I began to notice that my son was kicking balls farther than I was hitting them. I also realized that I was going about this all wrong. *If he is to acquire a love for sports,* I thought, *perhaps he should watch someone who knows what they're doing.*

And so it was, a few days later, that we found ourselves in the middle of several thousand baseball fans searching for a glimmer of hope in a 9–1 thrashing of the home team.

"See, Stephen, there's the pitcher. He's looking at the catcher, and the catcher's going to wiggle his fingers."

"Huh?"

"He's telling the pitcher what kind of pitch to throw. You watch now."

My son is watching all right. He is watching the man with a huge box on his head move slowly toward us, his megaphone voice stuck on, "GET YOUR POPCORN, PEANUTS, CANDIES, BEER . . ."

"Daddy, what's beer?"

"Uh, well, son beer is . . ." His attention is diverted to the mascot. The catlike creature is coming our way, surrounded by dozens of kids hoping for a hug. Stephen shrinks into the seat beside me. "I don't like him," he says. But boy does he like the food. And there is lots of it: popcorn, peanuts, orange pop. And there's only a 300 percent markup. As my money runs out and the score reaches 11–1, we head for the exit.

It has been a big day for a little boy, but as we point our Ford homeward he has yet to run out of questions. The boy moves the conversation from ice cream to beer, from baseball to lions. And finally to Jesus.

Since my best friend's only daughter was killed in a car accident a few months ago, his questions astound me. "Daddy, if Janella is in heaven," he asks, "does she have nail scars in her hands?"

"No," I explain, "Jesus got nail scars in His hands so we wouldn't have to. Janella is with Jesus . . . I wonder if she's seen His scars yet."

The boy is not through: "If good guys go to heaven, where do bad guys go?"

"Well . . . remember the verse we've been saying at bedtime? 'For God so loved the world, that He gave His one and only Son, that whoever believes in Him shall not perish but have eternal life'?" He helps me finish it. "Well, when we believe that Jesus died for our sins, He writes our names down in His book and we will go to live with Him when we die."

"But where do bad guys go?" Stephen rarely listens this carefully.

"Another verse in the Bible says that those who don't have their names in God's book will go to a place called hell."

"What's a hell?"

"Well, it will be the saddest place possible, because Jesus won't be there."

"I don't wanna go there."

"You don't have to. You can go to heaven."

"How?"

"Just tell Jesus you're sorry you're a sinner. Have you done bad things?"

He pauses. "I pulled the head off Rachael's doll and put it in the garbage."

I pause. "Well . . . you can tell God you're sorry. And that you're glad He died for your sins. And you can ask Him to come into your life and help you live the way He wants you to live."

"Okay. You help me."

By the time we finish praying, my heart is soaring.

"Play Scott Wesley Brown, Daddy."

I reach for the tape deck.

"Glory, hallelujah, look what God is doing," Scott sings. Stephen taps his feet, and a tear finds its way down my cheek. This is one of those moments parents never forget. A moment parents pray for. A moment that causes angels to party and names to be written down. Signed in blood. Forever.

I can hear some of you say that Stephen is too young. That a four-year-old can't know enough to make an eternal decision. Perhaps you are right. But I believe he will renew that commitment as he understands more about it. And for now I'm thankful he has obeyed a voice that still beckons to all of us: "Unless you become like little children, you will never enter the kingdom of heaven."

That night as I tuck him in and pray with him, he's not quite through with his questions.

"Daddy, will we play baseball in heaven?" Stephen's favorite song has finished, but not his questions.

"Would you like that?"

"Uh huh."

"I think we will. And maybe we'll golf, too. But I learned something today, Stephen. You know what?"

"What?"

"I learned that there are things much better than baseball. You see, baseball only goes nine innings, and somebody always loses. Heaven will last forever, and you only win there."

"I like that," he says.

"Me, too. And . . . Stephen . . . you'll have to talk to Rachael. About her dolly."

He raises his eyebrows, then smiles. "Okay," he says. And moments later as I sit beside him stroking his hair, the newest kid in the Kingdom falls fast asleep.

Happy Holidays

Until last week I have always looked forward to summer vacation. In fact, as a boy I began looking forward to it in early September, about the time Mr. Kowalski started handing out those math assignments. By the time July arrived, my father had developed a highly sophisticated method of choosing our vacation destination. Once we packed, he would drive to a major intersection in our small town, then take a vote. "How many want to go left?" he'd say. "How many want to go right?" Sometimes we'd end up in Billings, Montana, and sometimes in Nome, Alaska (Nome was one of a very few places we had no relatives, so we didn't stay there long).

We also had a method for car travel. Dad's personal goal was to make it across Canada without stopping at any restrooms. Every few hours, we'd tell Dad that we had "to go," but he would say, "Eh? Did you say something? My hearing hasn't been the same since The War." Once Mom reached over, turned the car off, and we coasted into the nearest service station. Dad didn't say a thing. Every once in a while my mother would offer to drive, knowing that

Dad would not let her unless he went blind in both eyes and suffered a heart attack. On these trips, my sister and I did not always see eye to eye, either. We sat in the back seat pinching and poking, and to this day when I think of miracles I think of the fact that my parents did not lock us both in the trunk and abandon the car.

This past May, believing that preparation is the key to peace, I carefully planned our family vacation in advance. I found a brochure with the perfect title: "Horizon Bed and Breakfast. Join us for the rest of your life." On the cover was a picturesque cottage by a lake. "Nestled deep in the heart of the Canadian Rockies," the brochure boasted, "you will find yourself walking barefoot through cherry orchards, admiring breath-taking sunsets, strolling the beaches and enjoying the waterslides." When I saw that the nearby restaurants included McDonald's, the deal was done. What more did we need?

I showed it to my wife, who had just been attacked by a small child who was snacking on peanut butter. "What do you think?" I asked.

"I think it's a great idea," she said. "After last year, you could use a rest."

I dialed the number.

"Yes," said a voice in my earpiece, "we have a vacancy in July . . . what's that? Oh sure. Bring the kids. They'll love it here. We're on a small farm. There are some cows, some swings . . . What's that? . . . no, no bears. At least I haven't seen any bears . . . HAVE YOU SEEN ANY BEARS, HONEY? No, no bears. Cows, though . . . What's that? . . . Let me check. IS THE HOUSE CHILDPROOF,

DEAR? Yes. It's childproof. We've had kids stay here before. Besides, we have grandchildren, you know."

"We'll take it." Hanging the phone up, I turned to my wife, "It's childproof," I said. "Like Fort Knox. Or Alcatraz."

When July came, our family of five headed down the highway toward a cozy, childproof cabin in the mountains. "Do you remember vacations before we had kids?" I asked Ramona. "How we used to have room in the car. Music we liked. No need for ear plugs." And I got to thinking about my own personal enjoyment. About my need for a rest. *We diaper the kids,* I thought, *but sometimes I need to be pampered, too.*

"Did we forget anything?" I asked out loud.

"Like what?"

"Like diapers?"

"No. We brought diapers."

"What about *extra* diapers?"

"Yep. We brought extra diapers."

"What about extra-*thick* diapers?"

"Yep. Extra-thick diapers."

"Uh, games? Cassettes? Books? Lego blocks? Stuffed animals? Sliced apples?"

"Yep."

"What about the kids?" I said. "Did we bring the kids?"

Three hundred potty stops later, as night began to fall, we arrived in one of the most beautiful spots on the face of the earth. It was better than the brochure. *Callaway,* I thought to myself, *if you can't sleep here, you can't sleep anywhere.*

"Let me sleep in," I said to my wife, as we climbed into bed, "I need the rest."

"CRASH!" It is the morning now, and I sit up straight in bed. "What was that?" Bleary-eyed, I walk downstairs to the crime scene. Rachael, our two-year-old, is okay, but she is looking up at me with an innocent grin.

"What happened, Rachael?"

"Nuffin."

But behind her is evidence that something *did* happen. Behind her are the pieces of a priceless cowboy statue. Or at least it used to be priceless. "What were you doing?" I ask, angrily.

"Bang!" she uses her hands to tell me.

Now, it is one thing to smash priceless things at home—this has been done—but when you are a guest . . . "I guess we just bought a statue," I say out loud.

Back in our room I am angry. Very angry. A short night and eight hours on the road have left us all a little run-down. Now this. Let me see, whom shall I blame? Ramona comes into the room. "Where were you?" I ask.

"The boys almost got trampled by a cow!"

"I've looked forward to this holiday for weeks, now look what happens! Those things are worth HUNDREDS OF DOLLARS."

"Cows?"

"No, horse statues."

"You're blaming me?"

"I thought you were watching her."

"I was," she explains. "But I can't be everywhere. It's 10 o'clock. Where were you?"

"In bed," I said, "I'm tired. It was a long drive."

"You wouldn't let me drive," she said. "And you know something? You're always like this on holidays. Why don't you relax? Lighten up a little. We're having breakfast, then going to the waterslide."

Ah, yes, the waterslide. What can go wrong at a waterslide?

✻✻✻

"I'll take care of the kids, Ramona, why don't you get us some ice cream?" We have spent an hour in the sun, but my thoughts are still ice-cold.

In the children's section of the waterslide are three shallow kids' pools, one at the top, one at the bottom, and one in between. Each is surrounded by white rocks, and all are connected by slides. "Stephen," I say to my eldest, "you take Rachael and Jeffrey to the top pool and send them down the slide. I'll catch 'em." General Phil is barking orders.

"Okay," he says. It's simple enough.

Standing in the bottom pool, water up to my knees, I almost enjoy the sight of the three of them going hand in hand up the sidewalk. When they arrive at the top pool I yell, "All right, let her go."

Stephen picks Rachael up and lets her go—down the wrong slide! I lunge from the pool, run over the rocks and jump to catch her—just in time. She is grinning from ear to ear. The lifeguard shouts, "Hey, you there, stay off the rocks."

"Daddy, funny," Rachael says. I don't think it's funny at all.

Looking up, I notice that Stephen is now inserting his little brother in the *other* slide. The *wrong* slide. "No, Stephen. Don't let him go!" I yell.

He lets him go.

Down comes Jeffrey . . . on his back . . . heading for the bottom pool . . . watching the sky race by. I splash my way from the middle pool, fall flat on my jeans, then climb over the rocks again. Instant replay.

"HEY!" screams the lifeguard, "DON'T RUN ON THE ROCKS!" The paying public stops to watch. "Crazy guy," says the one in the fluorescent green trunks.

I am fuming as I crash into the bottom pool. Jeffrey is already one foot under, his wide eyes watching as I frantically pull him out. "Jeffrey, are you okay?" He coughs twice and smiles as if to say, "What's all the fuss, Dad? Hey, it's the holidays!"

❦❦❦

As I write this, our vacation is over. Early. It seems we hadn't budgeted for a $300 bronze-colored horse statue. I guess I needed the time to help my father fix the statue anyway. It sits across the room now, held together by glue and paint that's not quite the right color. Looking at it now, I realize that perhaps . . . just maybe, the statue was worth every penny. You see, the rider sits beside his horse, playing the harmonica ("Home, Home on the Range") and staring at me. For the past few days whenever I look at him just right, he seems to talk to me. He speaks in a cowboy drawl and he says: "Hey, whadya expect, tenderfoot? Ya saddled up for this trek thinking only uh yourself, didn't ya?"

I hang my head.

"Ya think your wife's not tired, too? You shoulda' been thinkin' uh her, partner. And the little 'uns. Next time ya saddle up, think of the other riders first, it'll go better for ya, I guarantee."

I've thought of dropping this statue on the floor again. He talks too much. But I can't bring myself to do it.

He's talking again: "A man wrapped up in himself makes a mighty small package," he says.

And I think I'd better listen.

19

Party Training

On Tuesday morning, my wife and I, in our infinite wisdom, invited ten small boys to help us celebrate our son's birthday party. When I was a child I squeezed the front brakes on my three-speed bicycle while flying around a gravel corner. That was not a wise decision either.

Oh, the children enjoyed themselves all right. They spent the afternoon breaking water balloons over one another's tiny skulls, and when the clouds rolled in, they hustled out of the rain and began dismantling our dining room, starting with Great-Gramma's flowered china. Ramona and I scratched our heads, recalling the good old days way back when parents did not need to invite the entire neighborhood; when they could get away without presenting each guest with an expensive candy bag and perhaps a mutual fund or two.

According to recent statistics, however, the average parent will spend approximately three zillion dollars on birthday parties. And that's just for decorations. Some will hire clowns, rent theme parks, and employ petting zoos, complete with giraffes. I kid you not. A New York mother recently hired a ballet company to perform the *Nutcracker* suite for her six-year-old and six friends. I wonder what she'll do next year. One couple brainstormed on ways to freeze their pool over so they could bring in members of the Ice Capades. Children who are guests at parties these days get more presents than I did when I was the main attraction. Back when I was a kid, I was grateful if my parents remembered my birthday at all. And since there were five of us, I was sometimes glad if they remembered my name. If I sound angry about any of this, I want you to know that I AM NOT!

As a herd of ten-year-olds swarmed our table, inhaling gourmet hot dogs, Jeffrey opened a wide assortment of gifts. They included chocolate bars, Legos, water guns, a soccer ball, a basketball, and four gift certificates for video rentals. "We're bored," said the kids when the last gift was ripped. "Let's go get some movies."

I sat there remembering the last time Jeffrey attended a friend's birthday party/sleepover. His eyes were bloodshot for three days. "It was SO cool," he told me the next day. "We stayed up till four watching movies and playing Nintendo."

"Did you talk?" I asked him. "Did you do something together?"

"Nah," he said, "they had four TVs. It was really cool."

As we scraped plates and loaded the dishwasher, the boys pointed water pistols at me and demanded that we rent some movies. "Did you know that watching TV kills brain cells?" I asked. "You guys keep watching TV, you'll be dumber than Silly Putty. I didn't have TV when I was a kid. It's why I'm so smart."

They stared at me with wide eyes, as if they were seeing a real live dinosaur for the very first time. "You didn't have TV!" they gasped in amazement. "What did you do?"

"Played," I said. "Invented things. Used my head for more than a hat rack."

They hesitated momentarily, clearly making a decision. Then they said, "Let's watch a movie."

"Which one?"

They didn't know. They had seen most of them, but they could watch them again. They thought we should stand in the video store and look. I'd done that before. I didn't think it was a place for little boys.

And so I took them downstairs and lined them up in front of the dartboard. "Let's play pin the dart on your foreheads," I said. No one laughed. They sulked. They frowned. They thought of movies. And so I drew up a chart and cheered them on in the first-ever Jeffrey Callaway Invitational Dart Classic. Soon the smiles returned. When the ice cream came, they let it melt. Darts were better than ice cream. When the rain lifted, we headed to the back yard. "We're bored," they said once again. "Let's watch movies. Tons of them."

I said, "Let's play Pickle."

They hadn't heard of it. I told them we needed two blankets, a tennis ball, two baseball gloves, and their little bodies. We put a blanket at each end of the yard. Two of us donned gloves and stood on the blankets. I threw the ball in the air and yelled "POP FLY!" and the kids tried to get from one blanket to the other without being tagged. "If you're tagged out three times, you're finished," I hollered.

The game began. The kids screamed. They panicked. They laughed. They slid ten feet on wet grass, then they got up and ran like they'd been caught stealing raspberries.

"This is the most fun I've had in my life," panted one of them, after being tagged out for the third time. "This is the best party ever," wheezed another. And he meant it.

Later that night, after the children were tucked in, I sat downstairs thinking about parties and parenting. It's easy to give our children everything they want and nothing that they need, isn't it? We plunk them in front of one-eyed monsters that teach them things we never would. Believe me, I know. I've done it. It's easy. It's convenient. But it saps their creativity and deadens their souls. The best parties are the simplest ones. The ones where laughter is heard and games are played. Where children are loved and reminded to make the most of another year. My daughter's birthday is exactly one week away, so I think I'll remind my wife of these things.

In fact, that's her voice calling from upstairs.

She wants me to glue Gramma's flowered china back together.

CHAPTER

20

Deinonychus
and the Big Bang

Movie star Mel Gibson once said, "I don't think we crawled out of the mud some place. I think we were created." I may not look like Mel, but I agree with him. I am not a strong proponent of the theory of evolution either. Oh sure, I have taken my children to the zoo, and I must admit that there are definite similarities between the actions of certain of the species and the antics of certain of my off-spring. But, you see, my wife and I have applied the cornerstone of this same ideology to our children's rooms, and it simply does not work.

Just this morning, for instance, Ramona shut the door on the very area where the Big Bang itself had occurred. Hours later, she opened it, hoping to see our son's room cleaned, the walls painted, new carpeting, new furniture. But it was much the way he left it, and she did not have 360 million years to wait.

On the other hand, I don't have trouble believing that large reptiles called dinosaurs roamed the earth even before my high school teachers. In fact, we have one in our house at this very moment. He is in the hallway, two sharp claws on each front leg pointed menacingly at his little brother.

"Stephen, what are you doing?" I ask.

"Playin' dinosaurs," he growls fiercely. "I'm a deinonychus."

"What's Jeffrey?"

"He's a T. rex." More growling.

"They don't eat each other, do they?"

"Na, they just eat smaller dinosaurs. Like Rachael."

Our children's fixation with dinosaurs has come as no small shock to my mother. Since she was born with the same natural affection for reptiles that balloons have for porcupines, the following scene was played out often during my childhood.

ME: "Mother, lookee here."

MOM: "What is it, Philip?"

ME: "Uh, I found it out back. It's a salamander."

MOM: "AAAAAAAHHHHH!"

DAD: "Son, would you please go and get the smelling salts?"

My mother is no theologian. But she believes God should have told Adam and Eve not to eat the snake.

While you consider the historical implications of that one, allow me to say that I have endeavored to keep Mom's legacy for loathing lizards alive in our family, but it has been difficult to keep my own children from getting *into* dinosaurs.

It didn't help when a neighbor child (who shall remain anonymous, although for the sake of this book we'll call him

Joel McClanahan) discovered, after much excavation, that our "D" encyclopedia contained some startling pictures. Joel should have closed the book. Joel should have asked us to tape the pages shut. Instead, he showed the hideous pictures to my son. Since then, we have sheltered and fed an iguanodon, a triceratops, but mostly a deinonychus.

Deinonychuses, according to the latest treasure-trove of books my son brought home from the library, lived roughly 110 million years ago (give or take a few months). The creature had fighting claws on its feet and apparently became extinct from accidentally stabbing itself during meals. But they are very much alive for Stephen. He delights in telling me all about them, and he is so into dinosaurs that one day he came home from school with this poem:

> Deinonychus had a terrible claw,
>   He ate whatever he saw.
> If my mother said fine,
>   I'd have one named Cline,
>   To keep my big brother in line.

Unlike my son, my study of dinosaurs has done little to endear them to me. For one thing, I can rarely spell their names, let alone pronounce them. But I'm adjusting. I think. What I like best is tucking a gentle plant-eating baby brontosaurus into bed.

"Daddy, you didn't read me a story." It is bedtime in the land of children and dinosaurs. Baby Brontosaurus sits on the couch.

"I know, Stephen. You get a book. I'll read it to you." So as not to disappoint me, he brings his library book and cuddles up beside me. *All About Dinosaurs.*

Opening the book, I begin to read aloud: ". . . Many scientists now feel sure that birds developed from dinosaurs. They say that the dinosaurs did not entirely die out. Instead, they became the robins, crows, eagles, and other birds we see today. Dinosaurs probably live on today as birds."

I look down at my son. His nose is wrinkled. He is wearing his *Sure-Dad-you're-making-this-up-as-you-go* expression.

"Remember the robin we fed last summer? The one that used to sit in your hands. What was his name?"

"Gus-Gus."

"Do you think his great-grandparents were dinosaurs a long time ago?"

"Ha!" he answers, his wrinkle turning to a grin.

"Stephen, people have to make up funny things when they pretend there's no God. Some of them say we came from mud and monkeys. Do you think Grandpa looks like a monkey?"

"Um . . . ," the child scratches his head.

"Okay . . . bad question. What does the Bible say?"

"I don't know."

"In the beginning . . . what?"

"Um, God created the heavens and the earth."

"You're right. The Bible says that God made birds, the fish, the animals. And it says that He made you and me, too. Aren't you glad we came from God, not monkeys?"

"Yep. Did God make dinosaurs?" he asks.

"Oh yes, but I don't know if they looked exactly like the ones in this book."

"I like 'em," he says.

"And I like you, Stephen. Come with me. We have one more thing to do before I tuck you in." He takes my hand and off we go. A father and his baby brontosaurus.

Off to clean up the Big Bang.

21

TV or Not TV

I STILL DON'T KNOW who made it to the Super Bowl or who was ruthlessly exposed on *60 Minutes*. I don't know if Matlock finally lost a case or if aliens did the world a favor and beamed up the stars of *The X-Files*.

Two weeks ago, you see, we blew up our television.

It was bound to happen sooner or later. You see, Rachael came home from a friend's house that week. "What did you do?" I asked her.

"Watched movies."

"What kind of movies?"

"James Bond movies."

When my wife peeled me off the ceiling, we carved a new rule in stone: no movies until you phone home. Then I went over to her friend's house. And shoved potatoes up their exhaust pipe.

Two weeks ago I sat down with the boys to watch a harmless football game. For the 350th time, one of them had hidden the remote control. Before I could locate it, an ad for the latest horror movie had robbed the kids of three nights' rest. I stood to my feet, pushed the power button and calmly proclaimed: "Let's shoot the television. Let's blow it up right here. Right now. Let's blow it up real good." At first the children seemed rather excited. After all, they were not used to this kind of violence off the set. But when I confessed that I didn't have any dynamite and was merely going to unplug the tube, they weren't so sure.

"I can't live without it," said Jeffrey, who likes to watch.

"Me, too," agreed his older sister Rachael.

"I'll just die," said Stephen, clutching his chest and slumping to the carpet.

"Tell you what," I said, thinking quickly, "I'll give you something really special if we can go without TV or videos for two weeks."

"TWO WEEKS?" said Stephen.

"Two weeks."

"Will you give us a million dollars?" said Jeffrey the Dreamer.

"Not quite," I answered. "But how about a big-screen TV for your bedrooms!"

"Really?"

"Naw, but I'll tell you what. I'll double your allowance for a month. You'll be able to buy more candy and rot your teeth quicker. Then we'll have a big party in two weeks. We'll give you presents . . . toothpaste!"

"What kind of party?"

"Um . . . well . . . a fun kind of party."

"I know," said Stephen, standing to his feet. "A VIDEO party!"

Rachael returned to the room, holding one of her dolls close for comfort. "I don't think I'll make it," she told her doll.

🙊🙊🙊

I understand how they feel. I went without television once for 19 years, give or take a few days. We didn't have the thing in our home when I was a kid—except for the time my Uncle Clifford came to visit and smuggled in a tiny black-and-white from his RV. I was supposed to be in bed at the time, but instead I stood atop my bunk and watched through two strategically placed mirrors as John Wayne pulled a shiny six-shooter from his hip and shot a fellow pilgrim. This didn't happen much around our house, so I had trouble sleeping that night. Come to think of it, I didn't sleep a wink until the following Wednesday. During Mr. Kowalski's mathematics class.

On my eleventh birthday I asked my mother what was so wrong with television and if she could give me one good reason I couldn't have one in my bedroom. She came up with more than one. I believe they were in this order.

1. We are broke.
2. TV talks too much, but doesn't say enough.
3. TV is violent.
4. TV takes our minds off our minds.
5. You will learn more watching a lima bean grow than watching television.

"Television is the bland leading the bland," echoed my father from the couch. "If the knob marked 'brightness' turned up the intelligence level, I'd consider it, Sonny. But it's just the opposite. It's like Groucho Marx said: 'I find television very educational. When it's on I go into the other room and read a book.' I'm with Groucho. As for me and my family, we will go without it."

So we went to our friends' houses and watched their sets.

In ninth grade, on a rainy Sunday evening after church, as darkness began to cast its mantle on our small town, I sat in a friend's living room and watched both hours of "Jaws," a film in which director Steven Spielberg coaxes the entire cast to don swimming suits and become shark bait. I walked home alone that night, and on the way I vowed that I would not enter a lake or a swimming pool that summer. Nor would I take a bath. And if I had to shower, I would keep at least one eye on the drain at all times.

※※※

It's been two weeks now since we unplugged. As I write, the kids are still alive and playing semi-quietly in the living room, their backs toward the darkened set. In a few minutes we will pull pizza from the oven and celebrate two weeks without TV. Then I will remind them of the last 14 days, days which are best summarized with the following chart:

Who	What they gave up	What they replaced it with
Phil	Watching football, baseball, hockey, lawn darts, ping pong	Playing sports with kids, talking to wife, writing about not watching TV
Ramona	Religious TV	Radio, music, reading, friends
Stephen	Cartoons	Reading, hitting brother, saying sorry, reading to brother
Rachael	Cartoons	Drawing cartoons
Jeffrey	Cartoons	Playing with Lego blocks, thinking about cartoons

After we consume the pizza, the children will each receive a computer-generated certificate that looks like this:

This is to certify that
(insert name of deprived child here)
went 14 days without watching television . . .
. . . and lived to tell about it.
Waytago Kiddo! Yahoo!
(parent's signature)

During the past two weeks, I've seen some changes in my kids. And I've seen some changes in me. To be honest, I've missed the sports, but for the most part, not watching television has freed up time for better things. Things like wrestling with the kids. Reading good books together. And loving my wife. I've also had time to do some meditating on verses like: ". . . Whatever is true, whatever is noble, whatever is right . . . it won't get high ratings on prime time" (Callaway Revised Version). And I've even had time to print off a little computer-generated certificate for myself:

"I will walk in my house with a blameless heart. I will set before my eyes no vile thing" (Psalm 101:3).

Strangely, I'm more convinced than ever that I can accomplish this without unplugging the TV. Or blowing it up. That I can walk before God with a blameless heart by careful attention to daily discernment. By listening to the right voices. By modeling for my children that black and white can still be found in a gray world.

Now, I'd better go. The Super Bowl is on, and I finally found the remote control. It was in the sandbox.

22

The Trouble with Genesis

WE'VE HAD TO lay down the law at our house: No more Bible reading before six A.M. That's right, it was getting out of hand. It all started on a winter morning when our son Stephen was three years old and learning to count. He had worked his way up to 10, then 20, and finally to 99. At this point his face grew wrinkled. What now? Where to from here? I made a mistake then. I told him where to find 100. And how to start all over again . . . 101, 102 . . .

"See how high you can get," I said, not knowing that this is torture for the type of child who cannot resist a challenge.

By evening he had hit 999 and was looking for more. I told him how to find it. And how to start all over again. That night he didn't sleep much. "I'm at 3,007," he told me the next morning. By mid-week he had topped the 10,000 mark, by the weekend 20,000. He would fall asleep counting, he would fall asleep eating, he would fall asleep walking down the sidewalk. Thanks to me, the child was a mess. At this rate he would need counseling in kinder-garten.

The problem worsened as he entered school, journeying past Dick and Jane and into grade two where they string words together into actual sentences. One day not long ago he rushed home carrying a library book on dinosaurs. Opening to page one, he began to read: "Fifty . . . um . . . billion . . . years ago . . ."

"I'll tell you what," I said, "You read the book of Genesis and I'll buy you a brand-new pair of ice skates." He looked up from his book. "Ice skates?"

"Yeah, ice skates. Size 2." He thought he'd won the lottery. The child wolfed down his supper, threw on his jammies, and clambered into bed early. Believe me, this does not happen often at our house. Once in bed, the child began to read aloud:

"In . . . the . . . um . . . beginning . . . um . . . God . . . created . . . the . . . um . . . heavens . . . and . . . the . . . um . . . earth."

Ah, I thought to myself, *my wallet is safe. After all, the boy is seven. Genesis is fifty chapters. At this rate he will finish sometime during his sophomore year of college. What good will size two ice skates be then?*

A few hours later I fell asleep, entertaining nostalgic dreams of the time my own father (who is part Scottish) talked me into reading the New Testament. The reward was a coveted digital watch, and, upon finishing Revelation, I showed up to claim the prize. "Aha," said Dad, turning the dream to a nightmare, "You read it in English, didn't you. I told you to read the original Greek."

The awful nightmare is interrupted by a seven-year-old standing at the foot of my bed holding a big red *Illustrated Children's Bible,* and smiling proudly. "Daddy, guess what? I'm on chapter six!"

"Uh . . . that's really good, Stephen. What time is it?" Turning my head I am confronted with the awful truth: It is 4:03 A.M. Mountain Standard Time. "What in the world? . . . Stephen, you go back to bed and go to sleep."

The child obeys—or at least partly. He goes to bed, but not to sleep. By the time I enter his room at 6:30, he has been on a cruise with Noah, climbed a mountain with Abraham, breathed the sulfur of Sodom and Gomorrah, and learned all he will need to know about circumcision. As I sit down beside him he's zeroing in on chapter 25. "Dad, what's a Hittite?"

The next morning is much the same. By four A.M. Jacob has stolen Esau's blessing. By five Joseph's wicked brothers have sold him to Egypt. By six they have been forgiven—and by seven Stephen is as miserable a little boy as you will meet.

"Jeffrey, you stole my Lego!" he hollers, waking me from slumber. Then I am greeted with the sounds of him pounding on his little brother. "You give it back!" Jeffrey screams a response and the fight is on. "It's mine!" "No it ain't! It's mine!"

Normally, as the first rays of morning sneak through our blind and gently usher in a new day, I like to spend a few minutes quietly considering the opportunities that lie ahead; thanking God for a lovely rest, a new start, another

chance to serve Him. This morning all I can think of is
sulfur. "He's been reading about divine judgment, Lord. I'll
illustrate it for him." Hurrying down the hall, I command
Stephen into my study. "Bring the spoon," I thunder, causing Jeffrey to scurry under a blanket.

Before using the spoon, I have made it a habit over the
years to take a few moments to relax. To simmer down. To
put things in perspective. To practice my stroke. Sometimes
these moments are *very* few, but today they are many. Why?
Because, as I hold a small boy on my lap, I realize that it's
tough to spank someone when you are partners in crime.
You see, since I was old enough to read I've found the
Bible fascinating. But it's always been easier to enjoy it as
literature than to let it change my life. I've read Jesus' words
"Love your neighbor as yourself," and just like Stephen,
I've pounded on those around me. Not with my fists, but
worse: with my words. With my gossip. I'm still learning
that there is no virtue in reading about Abraham's obedience. I must obey his God. There is no virtue in studying
Jesus' words. I must put them into practice. A verse somewhere in the book of James comes to mind, "Do not
merely listen to the word, and so deceive yourselves. Do
what it says."

"Stephen, you're tired. I want you to say sorry to
Jeffrey, then get some sleep."

"Are you gonna spank me?"

"No. Right now I'm just gonna hug you. And I want
you to do something. I want you to remember that the
most miserable people I know are the ones who can tell
you all about the Bible without obeying it. I'm glad to see
you reading God's words, but that's not enough. You must
let them change you."

The following Monday, he received his ice skates. And I gave him a bookmark, too. It's covered with panda bears and the verse: "Love the Lord your God with all your heart and with all your soul and with all your mind . . . and your neighbor as yourself" (Matthew 22:37,39).

By Friday, Stephen was using it to mark his spot—in Leviticus.

Making Headlines

"DADDY, ARE WE RICH?"

It is Sunday afternoon. My son Stephen and I are sprawled on the couch, nursing cheese sandwich hangovers. For the last hour I've been reading aloud from C. S. Lewis' *Chronicles of Narnia,* while my son studies my face, clearly lapping up my every word. Or so I thought.

"Uh . . . rich? . . . well, let me think about that one, son." I haven't the heart to tell him that the buck has yet to stop at our house. And that, like my childhood dentist, he has hit a rather sensitive nerve. Just this morning Ramona informed me that our checking account is off balance, that the car is leaking oil, and that since Jeffrey threw up on the vacuum cleaner it hasn't been quite the same.

I go back to reading, understanding a little better why the children in the story wanted to escape England in search of another world.

"Daddy," Stephen is interrupting again. This time he's sitting up. "Daddy, you're getting old."

"Uh, why do you say that, Stephen?" I am calm, cool—sweating.

"You kinda look like Grandpa."

I set the book aside. My son. The one I have loved, sheltered, and clothed for more than five years. How shall I punish him? By sending him to his room until he's 21? That's it. I'll feed him through the keyhole. It was Mark Twain's cure for teenagers, but perhaps it will work for a five-year-old. This will solve other problems too: grocery bills, allowance, dating.

"What do you mean I look like Grandpa?"

"You have lines on your head."

"No I don't . . . do I?"

"Yep."

"Where?"

"Here, here, and here." The child is poking me, scrutinizing my countenance with bright blue eyes. "You're getting old, Dad."

Oh, boy. I didn't need these words this week. On Friday, we invited a few close friends over to watch me blow out 30 candles, or at least most of them. My "friends" presented me with a few gifts and lots of cards. Cards with inscriptions like these:

As you grow older, it's wise to avoid strenuous
activities . . .
Like trying on your old jeans!

Your age is starting to make headlines.
Don't worry. A good wig will cover them.

"Do you think I'm gonna die soon, Stephen?"

The child wrinkles his nose and ponders that one for a moment. "I don't know," he says. "How many are you?"

"I'm thirty. Thirty years old."

"How many's that?"

"Well, it's this many three times." I hold up my hands, all fingers outstretched. His blue eyes are bigger now.

"Wow!" he says, shaking his head slowly. "That's old."

Ah, my son, my son. What shall I do with you?

ｘ̆ｘ̆ｘ̆

Tonight I sit alone at the kitchen table, sipping hot chocolate and watching the sun set. It's taken awhile, but the truth is starting to sink in: I'm no longer a kid. No longer do I watch "the big guys" play football on TV. I *am* "the big guys." No longer do the neighborhood children call me "Phil." Recently they've taken to calling me "Mr. Callaway," and I find myself looking around for my dad.

There's nothing like having children to help us face our own mortality. They outgrow their socks quicker than we can wash them, and we find ourselves surprised at the change and aware that we are changing too, that the years are flying by, that we dare not spend our lives pursuing things we can't cram into our coffins.

The funny thing is, that's what has been bothering me all day: my lack of stuff. The fact that I don't have much to show for 30 years on planet earth. Sure, we have a car that's paid for. But I can't afford to fix it. I have a guitar. A stereo that sometimes works. But the house is a rental, and the cabin on the beach? Well, I drove by one once. No, three decades have not been kind to my wallet.

I don't have much in the way of fame, either. I've come close. I saw Clint Eastwood once—on TV. And I have a good friend who sat on a plane near Billy Graham.

"Daddy, are we rich?"

The answer is clear. Then again . . . maybe it isn't.

Getting up from the table, I put an empty mug in the sink and head down the hall to perform my nightly ritual: checking on the kids. Jeffrey is sleeping. One leg hangs out of his crib; the other is crushing his stuffed dog. How quickly he is growing. How quickly he is changing. It shouldn't surprise me, but it does. Quietly I rearrange his legs and cover him.

Rachael is awake, reading to Mary, her favorite doll. I tuck her in for the third time. "Good night, Rachael."

"Night," she says. "Love you."

From Stephen's room Twila Paris sings "Fix your eyes on Jesus . . ." but Stephen's eyes are shut. Turning off his tape, I sit down on the bed. He stirs, rolls over, and closes his eyes once again.

My son. What shall I leave you? Wealth? Not if wealth is measured in things you can touch. Happiness? Not if happiness is the absence of problems. But if wealth can't be found in a loving family, I don't know where to look. And as sure as happiness, peace, and satisfaction are worth searching for, I have found them through faith in Jesus Christ.

Yes, my son, we *are* rich. Rich in relationships. Rich in memories. Rich in fun. It may not look that good in the will, but when your face is cracked and you're approaching retirement at lightspeed, it's worth smiling about.

24

Eleven Habits of Highly Effective Parents

WHEN I WAS JUST A KID my mother told me, "Sonny, if you don't have the answer, ask someone who does." I was six months old at the time, so her advice has taken a while to sink in. Ten years ago when I took a job as editor of *Servant* magazine, I started a feature called "Innerview," which looked at the lives and thoughts of well-known people—experts—who don't mind tough questions. One reader wrote informing me that I should go back to fourth grade and learn how to spell "interview" ("Shame on you!" she said, wagging her pen), but for the most part, interviewing the experts has been one of the funnest things I get paid to do. Over the years, I've asked the experts for one practical tip on parenting. I think you'll enjoy 11 of their answers.

1. Live on your knees. Franklin Graham's teen years were characterized by drinking, fighting, confrontations with the police, and the patience, love, and prayers of his godly parents. Each night when he was out partying, his mother would pray for her prodigal's return. "She always sat up until I got home," recalls Franklin. "It really bugged me. I don't know how many times I tried to slip in late. There she would be, sitting in her rocker with a book or a Bible on her lap, and I knew she had been praying for me. 'Thank God you're all right,' she'd say. That was it. She never lectured or made threats. She kept the communication lines open, though," says Franklin. "She encouraged me. Told me to call collect anytime. And she let me know I was loved and welcome at home." In 1974, Ruth Graham's prayers were answered when Franklin knelt in a Jerusalem hotel room "sick and tired of being sick and tired." Putting out his cigarette, he got down on his knees and asked God to forgive and cleanse him. The years of running were over. The rebel finally had a cause.

2. Act your wage. The experts tell us that the leading cause of divorce is money trouble. Maybe that's why my wife and I are happily married. We don't have much. Larry Burkett, founder of Christian Financial Concepts and the author of a few dozen very helpful books, told me his unique remedy for the U.S. government's financial woes: "If I was President," says Larry, "I would hire a housewife with 4 children, living on $20,000 a year and put her in as the government budget director. She would straighten this mess out because she knows how to budget." Larry believes in the Ten Commandments. He also believes two more should be pasted to every fridge: Thou shalt spend less than thou earnest. If thy credit cards outspend thee, cut them off.

3. Don't always be right. Grammy Award–winning singer Steven Curtis Chapman believes that the five hardest words a man will ever say (apart from "You may marry my daughter") are, "I'm sorry. I was wrong." He also believes the words are essential to a healthy home atmosphere. "I would like to come to the end of my life," says Steven, "and have my wife say, 'I saw his failures. I saw him blow it, but his greatest desire was to live a life that honored Jesus Christ.' I hope my children will say I was a committed father. And it would be nice if people remembered a song here and there, but that's pretty insignificant compared to my desire to know Him."

4. Squeeze the day. Controversial author and speaker Tony Campolo reminded me to make the most of each day. "Too many parents teach their children to pray, 'If I should die before I wake,'" says Tony. "We should be praying that we'll wake before we die—that we'll make the most of each moment. The Bible says, 'Redeem the time.' Don't let life slip away from you. Now that I'm old, I want to pay more attention to each moment. I need God's help to live the rest of my years with the kind of intensity that only He can give. I want to laugh a lot and make others laugh. I want to enjoy my kids and play with my grandchildren. I want the time I spend with my wife to be rich."

5. Remember the three C's. Kathy Peel, contributing editor to *Family Circle* magazine, author, and mother of three, believes that parenting requires three C's: The first is *courage.* "We must have the courage to stand up for what's right and wrong. Parenting is not about winning a popularity contest. But when we say no to negative things we need to fill the vacuum with positive alternatives." Parents also need *commitment*. "I'm a babyboomer and our generation doesn't even know the word. When things get tough, we want to bolt, to jump into the next thing and find something or someone else. That's why half our marriages are ending in divorce. The good news is that God forgives us when we make mistakes. And we can make a commitment to stick with it where we are right now." Third, says Kathy, we need *consistency*. "We can preach to our kids all day about being careful what they put into their minds and then turn around and watch or read those same things ourselves. We must model the behavior we want our children to embrace."

6. Invest in friendship. When I asked Gordon McDonald, a pastor and the author of some of my favorite books, about moral failure in his life, he blamed only himself. But he did offer this insight: "What helps people survive and thrive is the accountability, support, and rebuke that come from being in a tightly knit group. I need men in my life who will look me square in the face and say, 'Gordon, at this point you're full of it.' And if I had had those men ten years ago, we wouldn't be talking about failure today."

7. Teach your kids to go MAD. When Ron Hutchcraft, who writes on parenting and speaks for the Billy Graham organization, told me these words, I said, "I can't print that, Ron." What he said next convinced me I should. "When my kids left for school in the morning," said Ron, "I challenged them to go mad!' What I meant was 'Go **M**ake **A** **D**ifference.' Not make money or make friends or good grades or good impressions, but impact their world. Children need a personal sense of mission about taking their friends with them to heaven. They need to experience on a daily basis a Jesus who is a real Member of the family. One who is talked to, talked about, and who has the deciding vote on how we handle our real-life situations. Family devotions are great, but they don't have the same impact as the integration of Jesus into our daily lives, where we take spontaneous, unstructured opportunities and turn them into teachable moments."

8. Teach your kids to sacrifice. For 18 years, Floyd McClung and his family lived in the red light district of Amsterdam, surrounded by pimps and prostitutes and pushers. Their mission was to tell these people the liberating gospel of Jesus Christ. "We believed," Floyd says, "that there were more pitfalls and dangers bringing up children in the apparent safety and serenity of suburbia, with one eye on the mortgage and the other on the VCR. Our kids need to see that we put obedience above comfort and righteousness above safety. Does God have our complete allegiance or is our primary question, 'What is safest, securest, softest, and most beautiful?'"

9. You don't always have to like your spouse. Popular singer Michael W. Smith's 18-year marriage to his wife Debbie is somewhat of a conundrum in the circles in which he travels. "In Los Angeles," says Michael, "they ask me how long I've been married and when I say eighteen years, they ask, 'Second wife? Third wife?' They can't believe she's my first and only." His formula for a thriving marriage is a bit foreign in L.A. as well. "The number one thing is to die to myself, which is a struggle every day. I'm married to this woman for life. And I love her, but sometimes I don't feel like loving her. She makes me mad, and I often don't agree with her. But I'm supposed to become more and more like Jesus Christ: to die to myself. I'm here to serve."

10. Keep it simple. During the past 35 years, Bill and Gloria Gaither have penned and performed some of gospel music's most cherished songs—more than 600 of them—produced 60 recordings and a dozen musicals, reared three children, and spoiled three grandchildren. They have also earned millions of dollars. When I asked Gloria what helped keep it all in perspective, she surprised me with her response: "Bill said way back at the very beginning of our marriage, 'All I need is just enough money to air-condition my house, and I'll never want anything else,' because he hates sleeping in the heat. We live in the same house that we built and moved into when our first child was eighteen months old."

Someone once asked Billy Graham how much money they should tithe. He answered, "I can't tell you that, but I can tell you this: If your standard of living isn't lower because of your giving than others who make what you make, you're not giving enough."

I asked Gloria what she would like on her tombstone. She didn't hesitate at all before saying: "She gave herself away for things that last forever."

11. Plan for your funeral. Patrick Morley, who has been the president or managing partner of 59 companies including one of Florida's largest, watched his empire crumble following a tax reform act. The crash brought him to his knees before God and to a redefinition of the word "success." "No amount of success at the office will account for failure at home," he told me. "Failure is succeeding at what doesn't really matter. I went to a funeral a few weeks ago, and I noticed this pecking order of sadness from the back of the church to the front. The only people who were weeping were the people in the front row. And I asked myself, 'Who is going to cry at my funeral?' Why do we give the most of our time to those who care about us the least and the least of our time to those who care about us the most?"

Good question. Patrick believes the single most important factor in teaching children a Christian worldview "is the way a father and mother live their private lives. A man ought to live his life in such a way that his children can tell that he has been with Jesus."

Since talking with the experts I've decided to do a few things differently. And I've decided, with Patrick, to plan for my funeral. How about you? Have you asked yourself who is going to cry at your funeral? Let me encourage you to spend some time hanging out with them.

25

Shearing My Little Lamb

IT'S GETTING LATE. The sun has gone to bed. So has my wife. The children, too. All, that is, except Rachael. Tonight, as I attempt to put the finishing touches on this section, she has brought her pillow to my study door (The Insomniacs Anonymous headquarters), hoping I'll take her in. The past few months have been like this.

"When you gonna put those games back on the computer?" Rachael asks, as I struggle for the last line in an important paragraph. Or "Come, I wanna show you someping." And so I go to see Rachael's "someping" and my paragraph remains unfinished. Or one of her brothers sneaks in and holds down the delete key.

What do you do with children like that? Cut their allowance?

Well, tonight I lay a soft blanket on the floor beside me, hold Rachael for a few minutes, then tuck her in. She is now conversing quietly with Kermit, a plastic toy that accompanied a Big Mac for only 49 cents.

It's been quite a week, this one. I call myself an author, but my children never let me forget that I am first a father.

On Tuesday we rented a children's video. I don't remember the title, but I can't forget the opening scene. Sitting on a blanket, trying to juggle popcorn, juice, and three children, we watched the screen as the young heroine marched angrily into her room and cut off her hair. After this the movie became quite enjoyable, but I wondered why Rachael wasn't there to enjoy it (normally we have to pry her off the television set with large steel instruments). While the rest of us watched the screen, she waddled out to the kitchen where we could hear her sweet voice, singing softly a selection of hymns. I had no reason to believe she was doing anything else.

Moments later she returned with a sheepish grin on her face and a pair of scissors in her hand. I say sheepish because she had just sheared her own wool. The left half of her hairdo was missing. Were it not for an unavoidable urge to laugh, I suppose I would have cried. Ah, how I loved that hair. I sat by and watched her mother trim it short and dump the long, blonde curls unceremoniously into the trash can.

"Rachael, don't you ever do that again."

"I won't, Mommy."

Then she picked up the scissors and went looking for her dolly.

Now Kermit lies on his back and Rachael's eyes are shut. I sit at the computer thinking about the events of the evening. About the influence a TV screen can have on a child. And about the impact of friends and peers and teachers and politicians. Of those who won't always have our children's best interests in mind.

Outside my open window all is quiet. In this rural setting we are spoiled by peacefulness. The only sounds at this hour are the occasional cricket and the click of my computer keyboard. Quietness. Stillness. Peace.

But I am not naïve enough to think that the quietness will last. We live in a world where, for now, wrong seems to overpower right. Where evil men and women literally sell their souls to buy the hearts, the minds, the bodies of our children. The thoughts have prompted a prayer that may not sound very spiritual but pretty much sums up the way I feel: "Lord, please protect my kids from idiots."

How about you? Have you ever prayed that prayer? Do you ever wonder what kind of grownups today's children will become after viewing thousands of acts of violence and adultery before they are old enough to clean their rooms? Do you ever wonder what kind of parents they will make when their only role models cared just enough to shed a tear as they walked out? Do you ever wonder how children can make eternal decisions surrounded by people who can't see beyond the moment? Let's face it, these can be frightening days for parents.

But they don't need to be.

Tonight I kneel beside my chair, right here in the study. Unfortunately, it usually takes thoughts like these to bring me to this position. "Oh, Lord, please give Ramona and me wisdom every day to write Your Word on the walls of our children's hearts. To show them Your love. To teach them discernment while they are still young. Thanks, Lord, that we can stand with our families on the edge of the unknown with nothing to fear and everything to hope for. And, Lord, thank You for all You are going to do."

On a soft blanket a little girl sleeps, and a Canadian winter is on the way. Getting up, I close the window and pick up Rachael. I wouldn't want her to catch a cold. She doesn't have quite as much wool as she did on Tuesday.

Shotgun Memories

Often when I speak I'm asked the question, "How do
you remember all these stories? All these details?
Sometimes I can't even remember my kids' names!"
"What stories?" I say. "You mean I told some stories?"
Seriously: I suppose my memory is so good because my
memories are so good. I had a mom and dad who loved
me, three brothers who paid me handsomely to get lost,
and a sister who cared so much for my eternal soul that
she often told me where it would go if I didn't behave
myself. Very little grass grew in our backyard. Football
and baseball games wouldn't let it. I had a bike to ride,
friends to play with, and secondhand bubble gum to
chew. On the coming pages are a few more things
I remember. I remember them well. It's tough to
forget stories of people who shape your life forever.

26

About Time

I AWOKE AND LAY STILL in the darkness. From my bed I could hear the tick tock of the living room clock. The enticing aroma of breakfast wound its way down the hall. It was early, but suddenly I was wide awake.

Morning was finally here. The morning of the hunt.

As we drove down the dusty gravel road that cold November day, I knew this would be no ordinary hunting trip. I had been hunting before, but today something was different. Today I was with Dad.

Alone.

Behind us lay the 12-gauge shotgun, brought out on special occasions such as this. In front of us lay what would become one of the most vivid memories of my life.

Being the youngest of five, it was a rare occasion when I could be alone with Dad. He worked hard six days a week and was gone many weekends. But today he was all mine. Today I was with the greatest hunter in the world. My real live hero. Someone who had not only tracked but shot, skinned, fried, and eaten an entire rabbit.

Driving along, I listened as he recounted in vivid detail previous hunting adventures. "Before you were born, I shot a pheasant over there . . . see that thicket? There's a pond on the other side. Ducks everywhere. Turn down that road and you'll start tripping over rabbits."

Outside, the cold prairie wind brought broad fluffy snowflakes to rest on the frozen ground, and the last few leaves struggled to release themselves from the grip of the tall poplar trees. But inside our car the sun was shining.

We entered the forest single file. I was careful not to step on any branches. He was careful not to get too far ahead. Adventure seemed to lurk behind every bush. "Sshhh," he would say, lifting his finger to his lips. "You never know . . ." And I was deathly quiet.

We ate our lunch of sandwiches standing in the cold. "Stomp your feet like this," Dad would say.

"But won't it scare the rabbits away?"

He smiled in response. "It will keep you warm. Besides, I haven't even seen a rabbit track all day."

"I'm cold," I said.

"Should we go home?"

"Sure."

Soon we were on our way. And although we didn't have a trophy to show for our trip, I didn't mind.

I had been with the hunter.

Years later, we were alone again as we drove down those same dusty roads. The shotgun was in the back seat, but this time it would serve a different purpose.

For weeks we had been watching the paper for just the right vehicle. Something old. And something cheap. We had finally found it in the form of a 1970 Ford Maverick, and now we hoped to claim the prize.

Arriving at the farmhouse, we carefully examined what was to become my very first car. And when it came time to pay up, Dad took out his precious shotgun and traded it in.

☆☆☆

As I sat up late watching these memories swirl through my mind, I wondered what it was that had made those times with Dad so special. Was it the thrill of the hunt? Or of buying my first car? No. The hunting trip wasn't very successful and, believe me, the car didn't last forever. But the memories would, because someone who had a "to do" list as long as my arm had taken the time to be alone with me. The love of an imperfect Dad had mirrored the perfect love of my Heavenly Father.

I thought of my own children, and of the times my son had tried to get my attention while I read the paper, or watched a hockey game. I thought of evenings at work. I had deadlines to meet. I was busy with important things. Wasn't I? I suppose I was. But that night, alone in the dark, I wondered just how important these things were. I wondered if anything in the world was more significant than the children God had given me.

Quietly I got out of bed and crept down the hallway to watch my three-year-old sleep. His face was tranquil, trusting, his arm clutched tightly around his brown and white teddy bear. What would he remember me for? My devotion

to my job? My love of books? Would he have trouble believing that God had time for him because I seldom did?
Tears came to my eyes.

"Lord, help me take the time. Time to hold his hand.
Time to walk with him. Time to talk with him. Time to
listen. Give me the presence of mind to put the paper
down. To switch off the game. To leave my work at the
office. To teach him about my loving Heavenly Father. To
somehow make it easier for him to know that You love
him because of the way I do. To show him that the most
important things in life cannot be purchased, they are gifts
from You."

※※※

On Monday, October 25, 1999, Danny De Armas was
in California when he learned that golfer Payne Stewart's
plane had gone down in South Dakota, killing all aboard.

It was a turning point in his life.

Four days earlier, at home in Florida, he had received a
phone call from Van Arden, the father of his son's best friend,
Ivan. "Hey," he said, "it's my forty-fifth birthday. Let's take
Ivan and your boy Seth out of school and go golfing."

Unfortunately, Danny had to decline. He was traveling
the next morning, and life had been a little hectic lately. So
Van Arden offered to take the boys himself. Danny hoped
to take them golfing someday, too, but not today. And so
the boys helped Van celebrate his forty-fifth birthday with
a day of golf at the Grand Cypress Resort. It was Ivan's
favorite thing to do with his dad. "It was a blast," Seth said
later. He ended up spending Friday and Saturday night at
the Ardens' home. They rode go-peds. And skateboards.

They even built a kid-made three-hole golf course in the front yard.

The following Monday, golfer Payne Stewart, known for his signature knickers, climbed aboard a Lear jet headed for Dallas—a flight that would plunge into a field in South Dakota, claiming the life of Payne and five others—including his agent . . . Ivan's dad, Van Arden.

On Tuesday morning Danny De Armas arrived back in Orlando. His son Seth told him that Ivan wanted to get out of the house for a while. There were too many people around, and he needed some space. So that afternoon Danny took the boys golfing. "It was my first chance to see the two of them on the golf course together," he says. "It was about time." As they played they talked about Van's slice and how he loved to let the boys drive the carts. They talked about life and death. And about friends.

On the way home Danny choked back the tears as the boys read aloud 30 cards that Ivan had received from friends at school. The car was filled with laughter as the boys admired the artwork of the friends. Each card tried in some way to ease the pain Ivan was feeling.

That night as Danny lay in bed, he contemplated his friend's death. And the startling reminder that we don't really have much to offer others in this life. But we can give them our time.

※※※

Recently researchers devised a way of attaching little microphones to toddlers' T-shirts, and began listening in on the conversations that went on in homes. They were shocked to discover that fathers spent an average of 37 seconds per day playing and talking with their children. Their direct interaction was limited to 2.7 encounters daily, lasting 10 to 15 seconds each.

Most dads I know don't need another guilt trip. But at times we need another wake-up call. I have yet to meet a father who came to the end of his life wishing he had spent more time with his computer. Or his newspaper. Or his television set. But I have met too many who seem to be spending the last half of their life regretting the first half.

It's not an easy balance, I know. We must make money to make a living. But remember that we must make memories to make a life. Will you start today? Tomorrow may be too late. Why not begin with a simple hug, a trip to the golf course, or a day in the country? You may even want to throw in a shotgun.

Larry Norman, My Mother, and Me

MY WIFE AND I are beginning to reach that uncomfortable stage of life when our children have decided that our music is not necessarily cool. Whereas they once found Willie Nelson's voice soothing, they wince now whenever they hear it, as if someone were drawing fingernails across a blackboard and dripping water on their foreheads. They prefer other music. For instance, I brought home a friend's album of blues music, which was composed by highly depressed people from Oregon who have not seen the sun since 1963. The words went something like this:

> My family they done left me
> My dog and cat left too
> There's a gallstone in my kidneys
> And my income tax is due.

The children loved it. They couldn't get enough of it. "Put on the kidney song!" they said, "Play it again!"

I can hardly wait till they're teenagers.

When I was a teen, there was nothing more important than music. Music came ahead of eating, sleeping, and sometimes hockey. Stephen Rendall and I would purchase the latest contemporary Christian albums, rush them home, tape them, then insert them into our car tape decks. How we prided ourselves on those tape decks. Who cared about the car? My 1970 rust-colored Ford Maverick had an engine that would not have powered my mother's sewing machine, let alone get me a speeding ticket. I didn't care. I had 100-watt speakers in the back window and the wisdom to know that no mere machinery can move you like music.

One day Stephen pulled up in his 1970 maroon Montego. Pin stripes. White walls. Genuine imitation sheepskin seatcovers.

"Climb in," he said, a grin connecting his ears.

I climbed in.

"Roll up your window."

I rolled it up.

Then, as we pulled away, he calmly inserted a Larry Norman tape, adjusted his sunglasses, and set the volume to 10.

Moments later our ears were pasted to the headrests with:

I was lost and blind then a Friend of mine
    came and took me by the hand.
And He led me to His kingdom
    that was in another land.
Now my life has changed it's rearranged,
    when I think of my past I feel so strange.

Wowie zowie well He saved my soul,
  He's the rock that doesn't roll.

"STEVE," I yelled.

"WHAT?"

"THAT'S GREAT! ABSOLUTELY GREAT!"

He turned the volume way down to 5. "You're gonna be late for what?"

"No, I said that's GREAT. Turn it up."

Now you must understand that I was reared in a conservative community where such practices were frowned upon. Where Larry Norman was often confused with Led Zeppelin and the Beatles. This so-called Christian music was shallow, we were told, and, at best, would cause us to lose our hearing. "You play that junk around the house," my trumpet teacher told me, "you'll kill your mother's plants."

"Ha, impossible," I responded, before disguising my Imperials albums in George Beverly Shea jackets.

"Listen to this," I said to Dave Adkins one afternoon, as we huddled near my brother Tim's stereo, hoping he wouldn't show up and murder us for touching his stuff. Nervously, I dropped the needle on the latest from the Imperials:

All we need is a little more time to get it together.
There's a whole lot of people been tryin' to get it together,
Like you and me—ooh ooh—that's all we need to be
  free, is a little more time to get it together."

"Wow," said Dave, "I didn't know George Beverly Shea sounded like that. He's hot!"

"And deep," said I. "Wow."

It was during those interesting days that I began play-ing music to another friend. My mother. Almost every night I would invite her into my room and attempt to cross her eyes with the latest from Chuck Girard, Phil Keaggy, The 2nd Chapter of Acts—even Petra. For some reason she always found time to pull up a chair and listen. I'm sure she rarely enjoyed my choices (just how much can a 55-year-old glean from "Lend an ear to a love song. Ooh ooh a love song. Let it take you, let it start"?), but she al-ways cared enough to listen. And she encouraged me when she heard something praiseworthy.

Sometimes my wife and I celebrate Nostalgia Night. After the kids are in bed, we pull out old record albums (are there any other kind?) and listen to songs that bring the memories flooding back. Memories of simpler times. Memories of hot cars and trumpet teachers. And of a mother who cared more for me than her plants. A mother who loved me enough to enter my world.

Tonight, as I reminisce, I realize again how much greater is the influence of one who cares. One who takes time. For, you see, she who yells loudest is not always heard the best. While many of my friends heard only, "Turn it down, turn it off, or throw it out!" I was privileged to have a mother with the wisdom to say, "If he's going to listen, I'd like to know what he's listening to."

Sometimes I miss those days. The talks after the music died down. Perhaps Mom does, too. Although she probably doesn't miss the music that much. At least not as much as I miss my hearing.

28

Goal of a Lifetime

I HAVE A CONFESSION to make. I'm a collector. When my wife cleans out the closet I stand nearby watching her every move and offering helpful suggestions. "Hey," I say, "you can't throw that sweater out, I wore it in fourth grade." If I had a flair for collecting things back when I wore that sweater, I would have a shoebox full of baseball and hockey cards. They'd be worth a fortune today.

As a writer I collect all sorts of clippings and stories and articles. In front of me is a shoebox full of infamous quotes from famous sports personalities. Here are a few of my favorites:

"If you slid into bases head first for twenty years, you'd be ugly, too." —Baseball's Pete Rose

"My wife made me a millionaire; I used to have three million." —Hockey superstar Bobby Hull

"I don't even let my daughter beat me at tic-tac-toe." —Pitcher Bobby Gibson

"All I want out of life is that when I walk down the street folks will say, 'There goes the greatest hitter who ever lived.'"   —Ted Williams, Baseball Hall of Famer

When I was a kid, I had the same aspirations as Ted Williams. All I wanted was for folks the world over to say, "There goes the greatest hockey player who ever lived."

When I was three years old my older brothers, in their finite wisdom, saw fit to introduce me to the sport of hockey. I had no idea what they were getting me into. I had no idea that my nose would be broken three times, that each of my ribs would be cracked (sometimes all at once), and that I would be knocked cuckoo seven times. Okay, I'm exaggerating there. I was only knocked out once. If I remember correctly.

For those of you who know little about hockey and so have yet to experience the joy of watching friends sign the casts on both of your legs, allow me to provide a little background. The word "hockey" finds its origins in a combination of the North American Indian word *tamahakee,* or "to chase with great speed," and *splochet,* French for "to bludgeon." It is a team sport played on a slippery surface with sharp blades, sharp sticks, a dangerous projectile called a puck, and not nearly enough padding. It is also the only legitimate sport since Roman rule which permits its participants to shishkebab opponents and, if caught, be made to spend two short minutes in a penalty box thinking about doing it again.

By tenth grade I had spent hundreds of hours on the ice. Practicing, practicing, practicing. I shot pucks at a sheet in the basement and at my brother in the backyard, and I shot them in my dreams. *If I practice enough,* I thought, *I will do something heroic one day. Yes, one day I shall score a goal so big I'll forget the broken nose, the stitches, and the uh . . . the uh . . . oh yes, the time I hit my head.*

That year my dream looked like it might keep its promise. Laying aside all individual goals, our team members had become a cohesive unit, confused the critics, and fearlessly shishkebabbed our way to the championship game. So, on a Saturday night in late March, the crowd (which consisted almost solely of teenage girls) packed our small arena to watch the stars come out. Peering in nervous awe through a crack in the locker room door, I had the distinct feeling that this would be *my* night. The night of the big goal. Yes, the years of practice were about to pay off.

But as the game progressed, the dream began to fade. In fact, as the clock ran down to the final minute, the dream had all the makings of a nightmare. We were behind 3–2.

Then, in a moment I'm sure someone somewhere still remembers, I took a pass from the corner and rifled the puck past a sprawling goalie. The girls went wild. The game was tied. And I was a hero—at least for the moment.

When overtime began, I had the distinct feeling that destiny was on my side. Call it premonition; call it intuition; call it ridiculous; for a late adolescent it was very real. Tonight would be *my* night and I knew it. Then, sure enough, about five minutes into overtime, I had my chance and I seized it. It was a moment that is forever available to me on instant replay and sometimes in slow motion. As the puck slid toward the open net, I dove, trying desperately to forge its destination. As the crowd rose to its feet, I swatted the puck across the goal line. The girls went wild. So did my opponents' mothers. But they weren't cheering for me. You see, I had just scored INTO MY OWN NET.

I don't remember much else then. I do remember making a beeline for the locker room where I sat down and threw a white towel over my head. And I recall the comments: "Don't worry about it, eh? Anyone coulda done that . . . if he was totally uncoordinated."

Through the muffled laughter, I hung up my skates. For good.

Upon arriving home that night, I headed straight for my room. A bad case of the flu had kept Dad from the game. I didn't want to make him sicker by telling him about my big goal. Maybe in three or four years he would be well enough to deal with the details. But Dad entered my room then, and I told him everything. I didn't dare look at his face. I could only stare at his red plaid housecoat.

When I finished, there was silence for a minute. Then he put his hand on my knee and began to laugh. And, you know what? I joined him.

It was the last thing either of us expected.

It was the very best thing.

You see, Dad was letting me know that my worth was in no way associated with winning a game. His message was crystal clear: "No matter what happens, I love you."

Wise is the parent who knows that life's biggest victories are never posted on a scoreboard. That shaping a life is more important than winning a game. That we learn far more from failure than success. Especially when it's accompanied by a good laugh.

More than 20 years have passed since the night Dad and I laughed together. And I'm just starting to realize that Dad gave me a gift far more valuable than anything you can cram into a shoebox. Something I'll never trade in or throw out. You see, the night Dad and I laughed together was the night I determined to skate again. In fact, I'm still skating. I've even scored a few goals over the years—in the right net. But none has been as memorable as that overtime goal, a lifelong reminder that the biggest victories can be found in the ruins of defeat. A lifelong reminder of my Heavenly Father's unfailing love for me.

29

My Loony Collection

JUST YESTERDAY, someone handed me the latest issue of *Forbes* magazine and flipped it open to a page that intrigued me. For the first time in history, said the page, the 400 richest Americans have a total net worth of $1 trillion, a figure greater than the gross domestic product of China . . . and my personal savings account. *Amazing,* I thought. We didn't have a whole lot of cash when I was a kid. When Mom and Dad were married, the banker asked Mom if she wanted to open a joint savings account with Dad. She said, "No, I'd rather open one with someone who has money."

Though we didn't have much of it, I developed a fond attraction to money when I was a kid. On Sundays my parents would entrust me with a small percentage of their small percentage, which I would jingle in my pocket all the way to church before dropping it loudly into the offering plate. Fellow worshippers nodded their approval. *A fine young man,* they thought, *learning to tithe 10 percent from his storehouse at such an early age.*

But as I grew in stature and deviousness, my enthusiasm for giving the stuff away began to dwindle. One Sunday I made the discovery that, with a little practice and much sleight of hand, I could pull the change from my pocket, combine it with a little from the offering bucket, and drop half of it back. This allowed me to improve my financial well-being with each passing Sabbath.

Stan Kirk liked me a lot in those days. He was my best friend every Monday. He would ask me how I was doing and tell me that he liked my hairdo. "You wanna go to the Dairy King after school?" he'd say. "My, you're sure lookin' fine today."

"Thanks," I said, pulling quarters from my jeans. "My mother gave me these. For chores. Yep. Wasn't easy doing all them chores. Laundry and stuff."

"Wow, your mom's cool!" he said. "Let's go blow it, eh?"

And we did. We *really* blew it. Fifty cents bought quite a cache of candy in the early 1970s. We felt like we'd discovered the mother lode. Candy necklaces. Mojos. Wafers heaped high with chocolate. By suppertime neither of us had much in the way of appetites and the sugar on my brain caused me to forget that mothers clean under boys' beds.

MOM: "Philip, what is this?"
ME: "Uh, that's A LOT of candy. May I have some?"
MOM: "I found it under your bed. Where did you get it?"
ME: "From Stan Kirk."
MOM: "Where did he get it?"
ME: "Um . . . maybe he found it?"
MOM: "Let's phone him and find out."

ME: "Um, well . . . actually . . . um . . . you know that money you gave me for the offering . . .?"

MOM: "Okay. Go get the strap, Philip."

At the tender age of 14, while working on a farm, I made a deal with God. After five or six hours of cleaning dusty grain bins without food, I became gravely ill, which is to say I discovered that cleaning granaries was not a vocation I wished to pursue. As I finished the last of the bins, I decided that, upon the farmer's soon arrival, I would inform him of my condition and he would compassionately rush me home where I could follow another calling.

But the farmer, whose watch had evidently fallen down a deep, dark hole, did not arrive. I waited. Then I waited some more. Lunchtime came. My employer, I'm sure, sat down to hours d'ouvres and roast beast, while I sat in a wheat field, chewing barley, and praying he would remember me. To pass the time, I tried to figure out how much I was making. At $3.00 an hour, I had already cleared 30 dollars (before taxes) by 4 P.M. By six o'clock, I began to make a deal with God. "Lord," I said quite loudly, as the sun began to dip beyond the hills, "I will pay back all of those quarters . . . with interest, and I will tithe ten percent of my earnings . . . if You will please remind the farmer to come and get me."

The farmer did not come.

"Lord," I said, I will tithe eleven percent if the farmer comes VERY SOON and has my supper in his pickup." By seven o'clock, the farmer had apparently found his watch and I had lost a very healthy portion of my earnings. For life.

Hoping to spare my children the trouble I'd had, I recently brought home a little container from a fabulous mission agency, Action International. The container says "Vacuum Packed" on top, which is a physical impossibility because of the large slit which accommodates coins. A label on the side makes clear its purpose: "Street Children Ministry. Help for needy children in developing countries."

From time to time we would let the children insert loose change in the slot until the can was quite full of loose pennies, nickels, and—if I got really generous—dimes. Once I even slipped in a quarter, but I was sure to withhold "loonies," our Canadian dollars, for my own private "Loony Collection."

"I read somewhere that Americans spend seven times as much on pet food as they give to missions," I tell my wife. "Let's do something about the average."

Ramona agrees wholeheartedly.

"How does it work, Daddy?" Rachael asks after planting a "welcome home" kiss on my ear.

"Well, this is where we'll put money to help some boys and girls who don't have as much as we do." Pulling some pennies and a nickel from my pocket, I hand them to her. "Here, put these in."

Soon all three kids are lined up. They insert the coins, then shake the container. Stephen looks disappointed. Nothing came out. No Coke. No chocolate bars.

"What will the boys and girls use 'em for?" asks Stephen.

"Some missionaries will buy them food and clothes," I reply.

Weeks pass. To my delight, the can slowly fills. Instead of buying certain things, the kids learn to put change in the container. What better way to teach them a lesson it has taken me decades to learn? Ah, the joy of giving.

Then one day: "Honey, have you seen my loonies? I put them right here in the cupboard."

Ramona turns and looks at me with a grin. "Well, the kids found them," she says. "And you've done such a good job of telling them about those needy children . . ."

And I think back to all those Sundays. And all that candy. And I know without a shadow of a doubt that God has a very good sense of humor.

30

Grandpa's Greatest Gift

SOFT VOICES WAKE ME this cold December morning. "Is it time yet, Dad? Is it time?" Outside our window a white quilt blankets the ground. Inside three excited children are pulling at my covers, hopping on bare feet, and calling through the darkness: "Come on, Dad, come on."

Ah, yes. Now I remember: It is Christmas day. It is also five A.M. But kids don't have clocks on Christmas morning. They have dreams, but their clocks aren't ticking. Dreams of chocolate and turkey and prohibited packages. Dreams which have a way of waking them early.

And so . . . down the hall we go, screeching to a halt before five stockings, concealing delectable and forbidden treasures.

"What about we eat 'em?" Jeffrey is three and speaks for the others.

"Not yet," I reply. "Wait till Mommy wakes up," and "Shhh."

We plug in the Christmas tree lights, then sit quietly on the couch. And while the world sleeps I tell them a tale

169

from my childhood. A tale of Christmas past, largely true, and translated here for grownups . . .

🕴🕴🕴

Once a year we children searched the skies for Grandpa. He always touched down during the Christmas season, so we would wait in the airport, our noses pressed against the frozen glass in painful anticipation. Soon, sure enough, the silver bird would appear, cutting through the clouds just for us.

Our tradition at this point was to whoop and holler until someone called security. We had good reason for the whooping: Grandpa always brought a gallon of genuine Canadian maple syrup and a brown leather suitcase heavy with brightly wrapped packages (mostly for my sister).

We loved Grandpa for other reasons, too. For one thing, he was the only one I knew who drank cough syrup straight from the bottle, oblivious to its high alcoholic content. Grandpa had a chronic cold it seemed, so he kept a bottle of the stuff handy, a bottle I once took a nip from, a nip I can taste to this day. I also admired Grandpa for his head. It was as smooth as polished brass—only it grew less hair. My brother Tim claimed the barber merely put a stainless steel bowl over Grandpa's head one day and said, "That'll be five bucks," but whatever the case, we couldn't get enough of running our hands over it and gazing at our reflections.

As a ten-year-old kid, I found church boring, monotonous sometimes. But never when Grandpa was there. If he didn't agree with the sermon, the preacher knew about it.

So did the congregation. During the hymn-singing, Grandpa searched hard for the right notes, but seldom found them. Of course, he didn't know this, and so he sang loudly, with vibrato, with feeling. Once I stood beside him while he sang, "Silent night, holy night, all is calm, all is bright . . ." He was singing this very loudly in the keys of F, G, and A, and a little girl in front of me, a little girl I had been attracted to since the Sunday school picnic back in May, turned her head and looked at me with one of Those Looks. I seized the opportunity and nodded in the direction of my friend's dad, blaming him. I've never quite forgotten her smile.

Grandpa Callaway was a big man, poundage-wise. Grandpa could never be found far from a box of chocolates, and the years had charged him for it. He reminded me of the three stages of a man's life: 1. He believes in Santa Claus. 2. He doesn't believe in Santa Claus. 3. He is Santa Claus. There were definite advantages to Grandpa's ample waistline. It was perfect to hide behind during certain games we'd play. And I suppose, best of all, the lap was big enough to seat all five of us to hear the Christmas story year after year.

But this year as we waited anxiously in the airport, Christmas took a turn for the worse. As the last of the passengers filed by us, it became clear that Grandpa's plane had arrived without him. This was cause for concern, particularly for us young ones who couldn't help but wonder where maple syrup went which didn't come down. Of course, we weren't concerned only with maple syrup. No, we were far more sensitive than that. We wondered where the presents were. So we waited and we watched. Other grandpas arrived to the hugs and kisses of kids like us. But not Grandpa Callaway.

Then Dad noticed someone off to one side. Could it be? He was the right size. He had the right face. But he also had hair.

"GRANDPA!" we yelled.

"What in the wor—?" said Dad.

"A wig . . ." replied Mom, her hand over her mouth, ". . . sort of."

Moments later a restroom mirror told Grandpa why he had escaped our notice. The wig was a good one. Expensive gray with streaks of black. But it was on sideways, the "Made in Canada" tag sloping neatly over his left ear. "Oh say," said Grandpa, over and over. "Oh say."

But the news did not get better. Grandpa's luggage, it seemed, had not made the journey with him. "OH SSSAY!" said Grandpa, through his false teeth.

As the ensuing commotion died down, I began to piece the implications together. No maple syrup. No brightly-wrapped presents. No chocolates, maybe. And then the strangest thing happened.

I realized it didn't matter.

Christmas would come without maple syrup. Christmas would come without presents. Games would be played. Songs would be sung. Stories would be told. And, much more, Grandpa would be there. He had brought us the best gift of all: *himself.*

Of course, Grandpa wasn't taking it quite so well. As we climbed into the car, I heard him mutter, "Oh say." And I watched him reach for the cough syrup.

✗✗✗

"Didn't you get anything at all?" asks Stephen, as my story draws to a close.

"Yes, we did. But I don't remember much about the presents. I just remember Grandpa."

"Did he tell you lots of stories?"

"Oh yes. He loved to tell stories. And he especially loved to read us the Christmas story—of the Light that came blazing into the world, landing in a most unusual place, just for us. Of the Son of God, in a barn. And he told us that God could have given us anything He wanted. But He gave us the best gift of all: *Himself.* That's what I hope you remember when you think of Christmas."

Above us, suspended from red string, is a row of Christmas cards. In the very center hangs my favorite:

"If our greatest need had been information,
  God would have sent us an educator.
If our greatest need had been technology,
  God would have sent us a scientist.
If our greatest need had been money,
  God would have sent us an economist.
If our greatest need had been pleasure,
  God would have sent us an entertainer.
But our greatest need was forgiveness,
  so God sent us a Savior!"

"Where's Grandpa now?" says Stephen.

"In heaven."

"He didn't sing so good, huh?" says Rachael.

"No, he couldn't. But he can now."

In the soft glow of the Christmas tree, Rachael and Stephen sit quietly, in wonder.

"Tell it again, Daddy," they say.

Jeffrey sits quietly, looking at the stockings, and wondering about something else. "What about we eat 'em," he says.

Speed Bumps

If you've ever attempted to divide one chocolate bar
among three toddlers, you know that humans are very
much concerned with fairness. But if you've visited a
hospital lately, if you've held your child's hand in the
dentist chair, or tip-toed with your spouse through
the valley of shadows, you know that life is not fair.
That it rarely turns out like we planned. One day
C. S. Lewis sat on his wife's deathbed, listening as she
strained her voice to utter these words: "There's nothing
like dying to make you realize you're not in charge."
Lewis thought for a moment, then responded wisely,
"Oh yes, there is. Loving someone does that, too."
Sometimes family life provides us with ample laughter.
And sometimes it is a reminder of how little we control
in this life. Here are some stories about life's speed
bumps. The small ones. And the big ones, too.

31

Flat Wallets, Full Hearts

FOR 30 YEARS he has been my father. I call him "Dad." His humor in tough times has been a wonder. His decades of faithfulness to my mother, an inspiration.

It's not hard, though, to find fault in Dad. For one thing, he worries too much: about his health, about his wife, about his finances. We tease him, but we all know he can't help it. Like poverty, worrying is hereditary. You get it from your kids.

When I was a kid, Dad and Mom made the decision to invest their lives in people. Instead of pursuing a handsome salary and a dream house, they entered the ministry. "Our wallets are flatter," Dad said one day, "but our hearts are fatter." I'm sure there are days when he doesn't feel that way.

A plaque hangs above Dad and Mom's bed: "Thou wilt keep him in perfect peace, whose mind is stayed on Thee because he trusteth in Thee." The words have hung there since I was born. Dad reads them often. Still he worries. Lately he's been worrying about the future. And he has his reasons. Though he's outlived a few of his doctors, his health isn't what he'd like it to be. The mobile home where

Mom and Dad raised us is getting too big for them now. The walls need paint. The hedge needs trimmed. The lawnmower needs replaced. And so they've begun checking out suites for the elderly. Small places. Quiet places. Away from the noise of the next generations. When I talk to Dad, he still loves to joke, but lately the tears seem to come easily.

***

It's 8:30 P.M. The kids are in bed and I'm finally able to turn on the game. The fourth quarter has begun, the wrong team is winning, and the phone rings. Relax. I'll get it.

"Hello . . . oh hi, Dad . . . Yeah, I just sat down to watch the game . . . Yes, they're losing again . . ." My voice trails off as he begins to tell me about his day. He's going to see the doctor soon, and for Dad dentist and doctor are synonyms.

Why now, Dad? I finally get a few minutes to take it easy and the phone rings. It's been a busy day. I was hoping to relax a little tonight. Can't you see I don't have time to talk?

". . . Well, you have yourself a good night, son."

"Thanks, Dad. Goodnight."

The next day begins early. I am swamped. There is work to be done. Important work. The Lord's work. If I don't do it, it won't get done.

When evening arrives, I am tired out. And the phone rings.

"Hi, Dad . . . Yes, I'm just reading to the kids."

"Well, I won't keep you then."

But he does keep me. He's not feeling very well, he says. I'll come and see him—maybe—I say. But I don't. And again I ask myself the same questions: *Why now? Can't he tell I'm busy?*

In the morning I'm back at it. Outside my office window snowflakes fall unnoticed, sirens sound, and there is a scurry of activity. An accident? A tragedy? I am too busy to care. After all, there are deadlines to meet, people to see, questions to ask. Once again I am comfortably entrenched at the center of my universe, all wrapped up in good intentions.

The phone rings.

"It's for you, Phil. It's your mom."

"Hi, Mom."

"Phil," her voice is wavering, "they've just taken Dad in the ambulance. I think it's a heart attack."

"Are you at home?"

"Yes," is all she can manage.

"I'll be right there."

Questions flood my mind during the five-minute run to their home. *Will I ever talk to him again? He doesn't phone that often; I should have known something was wrong. What if I would have . . . and what about Mom?*

On the way to the hospital, my mother is surprisingly calm. "It's true," she tells me, "God really does give us peace." I wish I could feel that peace right now. I've left too many things undone. Too many things unsaid. *Oh, Lord, give me another chance.*

We enter Dad's room. He is white as the sheets, wired to various machines. Mom reaches down and begins to rub his hands.

We talk, we pray, and the doctor arrives. "It's not as serious as we thought," he says. Sitting in the corner of the room, tears come as strangers to my eyes.

Dad: There are some things I need to say, before it's too late. You worry about your health and the future. And I have tritely told you that God will be there. But now I want to say that I will be there, too. Just as you were there to wipe my fevers away. Just as you left work early to watch me play hockey. As you took time for me, so I will for you. You can bank on it. As much as I'm able, I will face this thing we call aging with you. For someone who loves me as much as you do, it's the least I can do.

✿✿✿

When unexpected book royalties made it possible for us to make a down payment on our first house, my wife and I started flipping through house plans, hoping to build a place of our own. "Why don't we put a suite in it?" Ramona said, catching me off guard. "Your parents could live there."

"Right!" I said, then looked at her. She wasn't kidding. "I'm serious," she said. "They've been so good to us . . . if we can do it, I think we should." And so, over coffee and ice cream, we told Mom and Dad of our plans. Tears came once again to Dad's eyes. But before long, the tears were gone. Before long, Mom and Dad had moved into a custommade suite with a view. A suite with thick walls and strong locks. A suite they now call home. Of course the arrangement isn't perfect, but neither is life.

Often at night the kids disappear about bedtime. We're not too worried. The other night I went looking for them, and they were watching the Yankees beat the socks off the Blue Jays. Rachael was cuddled on the couch, studying the lines on Grandma's face. Stephen lay quietly on the carpet, chewing his fingernails. Jeffrey was sitting beside Grandpa, arguing for another channel.

I sat down on the couch and said a prayer of thanks: *Thanks Lord, for second chances. Thanks for taking care of us all. You've promised not to withhold any good thing from those who walk uprightly. Thanks for keeping your promises.*

The wrong team won that night, snuffing out our pennant hopes. But the score doesn't matter. Long after I've forgotten the outcome, I will remember that we were together. Long after I've forgotten who hit that final home run, I will remember that we laughed. That we talked. And that, while I had the chance, the right words were said.

❊❊❊

On my thirty-eighth birthday, I received a card from a man I've yet to meet in Halifax, Nova Scotia. *Aha, an invitation to a seafood feast,* I thought. But what I got was even better. Tom told me how much he enjoyed my book *Making Life Rich Without Any Money.* "I laughed, I laughed, and I cried," Tom wrote. "And that was just from looking at your picture."

Then he got serious.

"Eighteen years ago in my final year of Bible College I sent a birthday card with a beautiful red rose on the front to my 19-year-old sister. Inside I wrote:

"'My darling sister, I cannot afford to send you roses at this time, and if I could they would pass away. Unlike roses, my love for you will never pass away.'

"A day or two after receiving the card, she was killed in a tragic car crash. As I stood beside her coffin, I noticed all the flowers and I asked myself a question: Why don't people give flowers and praises and compliments while people are alive? That day I determined to pass out as many flowers as I could along the way. What a rewarding life it has been."

When we die we will leave behind everything we've inherited, everything we've earned, everything we've accumulated. But we can also leave behind some flowers. Flowers of encouragement. Flowers of grace. Flowers of hope. And when we do, we'll be able to say with Tom, what a rewarding life it has been.

32

Out of Control

ON A RATHER COLD and snowy day here in Alberta, Canada, I stepped out our front door, and slipped on some ice and ended up staring at the sky, which for a brief moment was full of stars, and stood slowly to my feet holding the lowest part of my back. Three teenage girls happened to be walking by at the time, and they stopped to watch me get up, and one of them asked if I was okay, and I said, "I think so," and my kidneys felt like they would explode from the sheer pain of trying to look like I wasn't experiencing any.

They kindly moved on down the sidewalk then without any outward sign of what they must have been feeling inwardly, and as I hobbled to work I couldn't help thinking about the tone of voice of the one who had asked, "Are you okay?" She sounded like she were talking to her great uncle Billy Bob who had never really been operating on all cyclinders.

I wanted to walk the girls to school, maybe carry their books effortlessly, and explain that I was a star athlete when

I was their age and that I am still in relatively good condition and quite coordinated for a guy my age. But I couldn't have caught up to them without crutches.

I suppose we've all had our moments of humiliation, and this wasn't my first. But it was perhaps a milestone in realizing just how funny it is that our biggest concern when we're in a great deal of pain is usually what other people are thinking of us.

One of my favorite high school teachers can identify. He used to interrupt perfectly good English classes with a crazed expression to remind us of the time he walked to the front of a huge church for a short speech. "There's something the Lord has been driving home to me lately," he began, as the capacity crowd leaned forward.

He paused for the sake of emphasis.

"I'll never forget it," he said.

There was only silence.

"Uh, I'll never forget it," he repeated.

Again silence.

Backing slowly from the microphone, he walked swiftly to his seat and unceremoniously sat down. Every time I slip on ice, walk into a lamppost, or drive my bicycle into a tree, I think of him.

Noah Webster showed remarkable restraint in defining embarrassment as "the state of being made self-conscious and uncomfortable." On paper it sounds fairly innocuous, but if Noah watched me go to work that morning, he'd change his tune. If Noah spent an entire evening at a gospel music concert with our children, he'd change his definition.

Since Noah died back in 1843, I realize we have a logistical problem here. But I'm still disappointed he wasn't there the other night when we unleashed our children on a rather large and unsuspecting audience of music lovers. Of course Noah was not in attendance, but if he were, his definition would now read:

em.bar.rass.ment (im!'bar.ᴄ.smᴇnt) *n.* **1.** The result of taking Jeffrey Callaway to a concert. **2.** The result of sitting near Jeffrey's parents at the concert. **3.** To disconcert.

Now you must understand that we didn't *have* to go to this concert. We could have spent a normal Thursday evening at home, reading to the children or climbing the walls with them. We had even considered a trip to the indoor waterslide (this my wife suggested before locking herself in the bathroom and laughing uncontrollably—for the reason see chapter 18). But when we heard that Steve Green was coming to town, we bought tickets. Steve's songs have been translated into a zillion languages, and I love his music. Besides, we reasoned, the children will gain a new appreciation for the great songs of the faith, and Steve controls a crowd so well. Three young children will not be a problem.

The show was nearing halftime when we realized we should have opted for the waterslide. Steve, in an act he had committed without a hitch a thousand times before, requested that the children join him at the front.

Proudly we watched Stephen, Rachael, and Jeffrey file onto the platform with about 40 others. Proudly we watched four-year-old Jeffrey loudly inform Mr. Green that "We have you on a movie." Rachael and Jeffrey even held hands as if they had rehearsed it at home. You should have seen them: their faces shining. Their blue eyes squinting as spotlights cast glorious halos about them. Ah, my father heart was proud. *Hey, those are my kids everybody! Our kids! The smiling ones. The ones with the halos.* Clearly this would be more relaxing than the Christmas program in which a three-year-old Rachael fanned the audience with her new red dress.

But relaxation was not on the program that evening.

As Mr. Green launched into the chorus of "God loves a cheerful giver, Ha ha ha ha ha," he realized two things: The audience had joined him on the "Ha ha" part, and he noticed that there were more "Ha ha's" than usual.

He also realized that MY SON was responsible.

You see, it had just become glaringly evident to 2,000 people that Jeffrey had to use the facilities located in the rear of the building. In short, Jeffrey had to go. Boy did he ever.

As his parents frantically searched for the word EXIT, Jeffrey performed a little dance which is quite cute when kept to the family room, but seldom performed except at Michael Jackson concerts. To the relief of all, the facilities were located in time, but not before the crowd was thrown into hysterics and Steve Green completely forgot his lines. (Steve told me later: "This was the first time I ever lost control of a concert." I told him: "Steve, you had him four minutes. We've had him four years.")

Upon arriving home that night, Ramona and I both confessed to feeling a little like I had the day three teenage girls sauntered off to school softly swapping jokes about me. Most of the audience in this small town knew whose child Jeffrey was. And one mother even told us that she was

embarrassed for us and that we should have done something sooner. "Like what?" I said. "Refuse the boy drinks
before concerts?"

As we reflected on the events of the evening, we realized that there's nothing quite like embarrassing moments
to remind us of our fragile egos. And perhaps more than
that, those moments remind us of how many things in this
life are beyond our control. We may not like it, but it's true.

It's true of our health.

It's true of our future.

And it's true, ultimately, of our children.

Slippery sidewalks remind us that we control less than
we think.

Later that night, I made the mistake of telling Ramona
about the teenagers, and we both laughed until we couldn't
stand up. It was the laughter of two who are learning to
commit the things they can't control to the One who controls all things.

A few chapters from now, you'll understand what I
mean.

👥👥👥

Oh yes, you're probably wondering how Jeffrey is taking the whole thing. Well, his favorite video is no longer
Peter Pan. It is Steve Green's *Hide 'Em in Your Heart, Volume
Two*. The child watches it now with a grin that grows
broader during "God Loves a Cheerful Giver." Perhaps he
enjoys the music. Perhaps he enjoys the singer. Or perhaps
he enjoys knowing that given the right situation, the right
audience, and a big drink of water, he could upstage him.

CHAPTER

33

Nightmare in Second Grade

I SUPPOSE IT ALL BEGAN way back in second grade when Miss Barzley came to town. Before Miss Barzley I didn't know how to spell terror. But after her first visit, the very sight of that white Health Department cruiser was enough to send our entire class scattering for seclusion in the nearby woods.

"I just saw The Car," Leslie Kolibaba would whisper, horror etched on his seven-year-old face. And we would tremble and clutch our arms and moan softly.

It wasn't always this way. The first time Miss Barzley came to town, we trusted her entirely. And so, like very young lambs, we were lined up single file in a darkened hallway and shot one by one.

I remember standing for the very first time near the back of the line, unsure of the results of reaching the front. Those who had gone on ahead were filing by with "attempted amputation" written all over their voices. "OOOOWWWW!" was how they put it, as they rolled down their sleeves. Oh,

188

how I longed for the hand of my father. He would show Miss Barzley.

But each of us entered The Room dreadfully alone.

Miss Barzley was a rather imposing figure, even without the needle in her hand. Large storehouses of fat (we nicknamed them Lester and Bob) hung like butterballs from her arms as she lifted them upward, squinting at the needle, and squeezing a few drops heavenward. Her smile was screwed tightly shut on her humorless face. The glasses on her nose were the thickest I'd ever seen, and she reminded me of a huge insect, a mosquito, I suppose. "Roll up your sleeve. It won't hurt," Miss Barzley lied. Then she poked us. It took just a moment, but we were scarred for life.

Once she finished, she handed me a sugar cube, the reward for not passing out. I tried to take two, but she spotted me with her big eyes and squashed me like a bug.

☥☥☥

Twenty-three years later, when my wife informed me that the time had arrived for our son, Stephen, to receive the shot some adult members of our civilized society have decided to give all five-year-olds, I volunteered to take him to the nurse. I was, after all, the obvious choice to comfort him. Having been poked myself, I knew what he was facing. I would hold his hand. Cringe with him. It's something brave fathers do these days.

"Will it hurt, Daddy?" We were on our way to the clinic now, and I had just informed my son of the reason. The tears came quickly as the news shattered his gentle world of cowboy games and toy guns.

"Well son," I said, remembering an old lie told me by a young dentist, "it will pinch a little."

"But what will they do?"

"They will put the needle into your arm, and it will come out at your knee."

"Naw," he laughed and began to wipe his tears. Anything Dad jokes about can't be too serious.

"If you are brave, we'll go out for a treat after."

It was enough, for the moment. But upon our arrival, events took a turn for the worse. Unlike the hallway of my experience, our surroundings were pleasant. And the nurse was slender and kind. But the needle was much the same shape of those decades ago, and Stephen was terrified.

Incentives to bravery were offered him: pencils that smell nice (as if children need another reason to chew them), stickers, a coloring book, more stickers, no-charge checking, retirement savings plans—anything, JUST RE-LAX, PLEASE! But he wouldn't relax, and at last the nurse asked me to hold the horrified child tight as she delivered the goods.

A month has passed. The pain has subsided, but not the memory. Today we are on our way to another clinic. Today we will have our warts removed—together. It seems fear is not the only thing he has inherited.

"What will they do?" asks Stephen.

"They will probably have to take our feet off to work on the warts," answers his dad.

"Naw," he laughs.

"Tell you what, son. I'll be there. Remember, I've got a wart, too. And if we are real brave," I say, "we will get a treat after."

At the clinic, Stephen is terrified again. My presence brings little comfort, my words even less. After all, I was of little help during the last encounter. Why should this be any different?

In the doctor's office we wait. The seasons come and go. Finally the doctor arrives with a bubbling vat of something.

"Sorry I'm late," he says.

"That's okay . . . are you sure there isn't something else you should be doing?"

Stephen is looking at the bubbling vat. His eyes are very wide. Like an insect.

"It's liquid nitrogen," says the doc. "Minus three hundred degrees."

Oh good, he's going to freeze our feet off.

"You go first, Phil."

"Uh, me? Um, okay, Doctor."

Slowly I remove my sock. He dips a long Q-Tip into the vat and rubs it on my wart. A little boy watches nervously, his eyes darting between my false smile and my afflicted foot. "See, son, it's gonna be okay."

When Stephen's turn arrives, he is relatively calm. He looks into my face as the doctor dips the Q-Tip. *Daddy can handle it,* the boy is thinking, *so can I.*

Minutes later, we are seated in a nearby restaurant. Our feet are a little tender, but our spirits are good. It's time for our "above and beyond the call of bravery" awards. We have selected the chocolate and raspberry variety. When they arrive, a little boy has some questions.

"Will our warts stay gone?"

"I think so."

"Did yours hurt?"

"A little bit."

"Mine hurt a lot . . . but you were there."

As we lick the last of the berries and ice cream, I tell him of Miss Barzley. Of waiting in a darkened hallway to get poked. Of her wobbly arms. Of her big eyes. And of the sharp needles. "Sometimes I wished my Dad could be there with me, Stephen."

Stephen has run out of ice cream and is eyeing the pop machine.

"Are you glad Daddy was there today?" I ask him.

"Yep." And then he adds, "I'm glad you got poked."

A door opened today. And I saw God in the words of my son. Because, you see, as much as I have marveled at the reality of Jesus Christ's presence in my life; as much as I have been comforted by His reassuring words; never before had I realized exactly why His suffering means so much to me.

God will never take us where He has not been.

As Isaiah put it, "He was pierced for our transgressions, he was crushed for our iniquities; the punishment that brought us peace was upon him, and by his wounds we are healed" (Isaiah 53:5).

Perhaps Stephen would say, "I'm glad He was poked."

Me too. And because of it, nothing will haunt us that He has not handled. Because He conquered death and fear and pain, we can look an uncertain future in the face. Because He was pierced, we have peace.

Whether you're standing in a hospital ward, in an empty house, or at the back of the line in a long, dark hallway, it's worth smiling about.

34

Journey into Trust

AMERICAN AIRLINES Flight 420. Blue sky. Early morning. Before me is takeoff. Beside me a beautiful blonde about my age. It hardly seems possible that we will spend the next few days alone. Hours ago we prayed with, kissed, and pulled the covers over three small children, leaving them in the care of friends (we hope they will still be our friends in 48 hours).

"It's great to get away from the kids," I tell my wife, "so we can talk about them."

"Welcome aboard, folks . . ." the captain is coming through more loudly than clearly as we taxi down the runway. *Shouldn't he quit talking and fly this thing?* I wonder as the wheels leave the ground. Apparently not. He is presently discussing the weather in Los Angeles.

Now there's something you should understand about me and airplanes. We don't mix. My brother-in-law was born on an airplane. He loves them. He is at one with airplanes. Airplanes and I are at two. If you were up here, you'd know that. White knuckles. Nervous feet. If you were up here, you'd know why. My own personal theory on air travel is that these things should not be able to leave the earth, on the grounds that they are metallic objects of enormous size and dimension filled with heavy suitcases, adult people, and airline food, which unless you are sitting in first class sneering at the rest of us, tastes even heavier than it looks.

A smiling flight attendant is listing the safety features of the aircraft. But no one is listening. For all we know she has just informed us that if we splash when we crash, our seats can be used as flotation devices . . . until the sharks get us. "Today we are featuring a student driver," she could be saying. "Some of those real pilots wanted way too much money . . . On this flight we are pleased to feature a smoking section . . . if you wish to smoke, please notify us and one of our stewards will be pleased to escort you to the wing of the aircraft."

I've been studying the wing of the aircraft since we took off, and I'm wondering if the guys who remove and clean such things know it wiggles as much as it does. I'm wondering if they replaced all the bolts. A movie plays on a tiny screen in front of us, something to prevent passengers from thinking, "Hey, I'm five miles above the earth in a plane built by the lowest bidder and piloted by a guy who speaks in a Southern drawl. A guy I've never met. Oh, I can hear him all right, but how do I know he can really be trusted? How do I know he isn't telling the co-pilot, 'Hey, who programmed this thing with Pac Man?'

Yes, if I could just see the pilot, I think I'd feel better. Reaching over, I take the hand of the blonde and close my eyes.

❧❧❧

I'll never forget the day she broke the news. At the time it couldn't mean much to a love-struck teenager. Merely another hazard of love down the road. But since her phone call that June day in 1980, the ever-present possibility has turned the years into a day-by-day journey into trust. A journey that has left me white-knuckled, wishing I could see the pilot.

"There's a disease in my family," she said across the phone lines. "It's called Huntington's. I . . . I just wanted you to know that, before we get—well—any further along."

I could tell the words were difficult, and I didn't know what to say. I only remember the strange feeling that grew in the pit of my stomach as she explained what it was.

"It's a genetic disorder that causes mental and physical deterioration." She paused, waiting for a reaction. There was only silence. "It's about the worst thing imaginable," she continued, "and it's fatal in the end—each of the seven kids in my family has a fifty percent chance of getting it."

I did three things while she was talking: I listened. I prayed. And I realized I'd better say something. "I'd like to marry you someday." My words were the last thing she expected. "I love you, Ramona."

Two years later, on a rainy but joyous day, we became man and wife.

❧❧❧

We are over Colorado now, experiencing what aviation people have chosen to call "turbulence." A 40-ish gentleman across the aisle is calling it something else. He is now in a horizontal position, dabbing clumsily at the spilled contents of a bottle of alcohol. I find myself wondering what his life is like. Are wine stains on his pants the worst of his problems? Or is he just like me, wishing he could see the Pilot, wondering what tomorrow will throw his way?

The turbulence worsens.

Ramona sits up and looks at me with a "Did-we-crash-yet-or-is-there-still-time-to-revise-the-will?" expression.

"Go back to sleep," I whisper, squeezing her hand. "It's going to be okay."

The turbulence has ended for now, and as we break through marshmallow clouds, a rainbow awaits.

Yes, it is going to be okay. Quite honestly, I don't always feel this way. At times my prayers hit the ceiling and land at my feet. Some days I give way to despair, and I wonder, "How is a happy ending possible?" But deep within me, I know the answer.

I know that God has yet to miss a runway.

That through sleepless nights His peace has provided proof of His presence. And that I can hold onto the promise of One who hasn't broken one yet: "For I am the Lord your God, who takes hold of your right hand and says to you, 'Do not fear, I will help you' " (Isaiah 41:13).

Yes, the same hands that shaped the universe are forging our future. The same hands that were pinned to a Roman cross are holding mine.

It's hard to believe, but when your knuckles are white and you can't see the Pilot, it's worth hanging on to.

35

Once Upon a Toothache

IN THE SPRINGTIME of my fourteenth year, I first experienced the hazards of tooth decay. In those days my mother baked potatoes by encasing them in tinfoil, setting the oven to 350°, and leaving them to sizzle for one hour or until the desired tenderness was achieved. This she measured by forking the potato dead-center and watching the steam rise. The method seemed to work, but for one small problem: The fork left behind small shards of tinfoil, which were a nuisance to eaters, and a dreadful torment to bad teeth. I experienced that torment one day after our family had gathered for a quiet dinner.

If you've ever had your ears pierced by someone whose aim was bad, you know the feeling . . . "AAAII-IEEE!" I said, holding the side of my head and closing my eyes.

"You don't like the food, Son?" asked Mom.

"AAAIIIEEE!" I replied.

"I believe it's his tooth," said Dad, with great discernment. "I'll call the dentist first thing in the morning."

I think it appropriate to note here that my father was, in most instances, a compassionate, rational man. But the next day he set aside these virtues, strapped me into our blue 1965 Pontiac, and pulled up before a red brick building on Main Street. Silver letters graced the front: "Harold's Dental Clinic, Ltd." We children knew it by another name: "Harold's House of Horrors."

Once inside, I was coaxed away from my father, down a gloomy hallway, and into The Chair. Moments later, Dr. Harold Pullman, D.D.S., arrived, bringing to mind the words my brothers had shared with me the previous night—as darkness descended upon our tiny town. According to them, Dr. Pullman was once addicted to laughing gas but had given that up in favor of alcohol. He now drank "like a fish" and was often "under the influence" while on duty. When confronted, he admitted the problem but assured those concerned that he drilled less accurately when sober, so the matter was still working its way to Town Council.

I remembered my brother's words as I sat in The Chair waiting for the good doctor. And by the time Dr. Pullman stood over me, wielding a sharp stainless steel instrument the size of a lamppost, I knew I was trapped. "Open wide," he said, as his assistant trained a spotlight into my eyes. "Hand me the D764 with a Honed Hook." He held out his hand, accepted the instrument, and began to probe.

"So, uh let's see here . . . uh yes, Philip, you've been experiencing some discomfort lately?"

"Yauush," I replied.

"Is it this one?"

"Nooo."

"This one?"

"Nooo."

"This one?"

"YAAAUUUSSSHHHH!"

"It's abscessed," said Dr. Pullman, peeling me carefully off the stuccoed ceiling. "Looks like we'll need to do a root canal. That ain't too great." The pain had dulled my hearing. All I could decipher was, "Roof panel" and "Let's amputate!"

Pushing myself out of the chair, I yelled: "DAD! HEEELP!"

Two decades have passed, but I still remember that amputation. Pain, it seems, is the one experience we humans relish only in retrospect. If you doubt me, just attend a parents' party on any given night. The ladies sit quietly on couches while the guys stand by the table, swirling ice cubes, and wondering what their wives are saying about them. In reality, they're not discussing husbandry at all. They're swapping scars.

JULIE: "My water broke 14 days before Joel was born."

ROSALIE: "No kidding. I thought Benno would never come. The labor lasted 23 hours."

SHARON: "I was *23 days* with our oldest! Then they took her by C-section!"

RUTH: "I don't remember a thing. They drugged me. I woke up when Timothy John was in third grade."

Meanwhile, the guys are discussing less violent activities. Like football.

※※※

Stephen, our seven-year-old, just had his first baked potato experience. Actually, he bit into an ice cube, which left a tooth hanging like a loose shingle from the roof of his mouth. What to do? If I leave it in, it may work loose while he sleeps, causing a major problem. If I take it out, well, how can I—without losing a finger? The parenting manuals don't cover this.

"Why don't you join the tooth and a doorknob with some fishing line?" suggests my wife, before scurrying from the room. "Then slam the door."

"Pardon me?"

She backpedals, then pokes her head around the corner. "My dad did that. It worked."

"He slammed the door on your head?"

"No, no. I stood in the corner and he slammed the door. My tooth hit the wall."

"What?"

"Never mind. I'll get The Stuff."

The Stuff is a little tube of gel that numbs what it touches. I put some on my tongue to see if it works. Yeth it doth. Then I apply some to Stephen's gums, and he immediately goes into orbit (this was not one of the side effects listed on the box). Apparently the pain has crept into his mind.

An hour passes, and we are no closer to the goal. At last I hold his head firmly and say, "We'll just have to leave it in there."

"Noooo."

As he hollers, I insert my thumb and push. The tooth breaks free. Stephen bites my finger, looks at me in horror, cups the tooth in both hands, and laughs with tears streaming down his face.

*   *   *

"Daddy, why do we have to hurt?" It is well past bedtime now, but Stephen can't sleep. The tooth under his pillow will turn into a dollar before morning, but he wants more for his trouble.

"That's a good question, son."

As his tongue darts in and out of the gap in his mouth, I search for an answer. How do you explain to a seven-year-old that the world is a cruel place where life is not fair? How do you explain that pain will come? That sometimes it will make way for a new tooth or a new baby, but just as often it will leave you strapped into The Chair with a spotlight in your eyes? How do you explain that we seldom grow without it? That, in the words of C.S. Lewis, "God whispers to us in our pleasures, speaks in our conscience, but shouts in our pains: it is his megaphone to rouse a deaf world."

The only thing that comes to mind is the story of my own amputation by Harold Pullman, D.D.S. So I tell him. He listens, enjoying himself immensely. Mechanically flicking his tongue. And smiling.

"You know, Stephen, one day our pain will be only a memory. The Bible tells us that God is preparing a place for us. When we get there, He will wipe every tear from our eyes. There will be no more death or crying or pain. You think about that next time you bite an ice cube."

"Okay."

"Now, you really need to get some sleep. Good night, son."

"Good night." The boy looks braver now. "Dad? How did he pull the tooth?"

"With a big silver thing."

"Did it hurt?"

"Oh yes. It hurt."

"Dad . . . um . . . I have two more of 'em."

"Two more of what?"

"Teeth. Loose ones."

"We'll look at 'em tomorrow, okay?"

"Yeah," he says, through the hole in his smile. "Tomorrow."

"Can you sleep, Stephen?"

"I think so." He is still flicking his tongue. "Dad?"

"Just one more question, son."

"Okay. Mom's the Tooth Fairy, isn't she?"

36

The Biggest
Surprise of My Life

"TELL ME, what has been the biggest surprise of your life?"

The question was asked by the host of a Chicago talk show. It was directed towards me. "Uh . . . my biggest surprise, sir?" I stammered, "I think it's your question."

Now that I've had time to think it over, I'd rephrase that slightly. I could easily mention our children. You see, we had them so fast that the anesthetic from the first birth was still working quite well during the third.

A friend wanted to know what it's like to have three kids in three years. I told him Ramona and I are far more satisfied than the guy with three million dollars.

"How so?"

"Well, the guy with three million wants more."

Seriously, each of our three has been a delight. To watch them grow. To witness the development of their spiritual gifts. Take Jeffrey, for instance. He's only four, but already he's exercising the gift of encouragement. Just the other day he was talking to a former friend of ours who has been struggling with her waistline. By her own admission she's been sneaking from fridge to fridge. From diet to diet. Apparently Jeffrey sensed her discouragement and determined to practice his gift in a most practical way. "Um," he said, "Did you know that dinosaurs are even bigger than you are?" And you wondered why I called her a *former* friend.

Yes, children have brought us their share of surprises. But if I were asked about the biggest surprise of my life, I would talk about something else.

Maybe I'd sift through my filing cabinet. It's full of interesting little clippings on various subjects. Let's see . . . Premillennialism . . . Quicksand . . . Rapture . . . aha, here we are: Surprise. The file isn't that thick, but here at the front are some absentee notices sent by creative parents and received by surprised teachers.

- I kept Monica at home today because she was not feeling too bright.
- Please excuse Paul from school yesterday. He had a stomach egg.
- The basement of our house got flooded where the children sleep, so they had to be evaporated.

My father can tell you all about surprises. He got one the other day when he arrived at our door and was greeted with those tender words every grandparent loves to hear: "Hi! Do you have any peppermints?" As Stephen and Grandpa sat on the couch chewing on some, Stephen was asked, "What would you like to be when you grow up?"

The seven year-old wrinkled his eyebrows and thought for a minute. "I'd like to play drums in a rock band," he said. "Like Petra."

After my 72-year-old father picked himself up off the carpet and uncrossed his eyes, he said, "Could Grandma and I come watch you?"

"Nope," responded Stephen, without skipping a beat, "You'll be dead." Sometimes children can be too honest.

"What has been the biggest surprise of your life?"

I suppose if Dad were on that Chicago talk show, he'd have no trouble answering the question. And now that I've had a little time to think it over, I'd have no trouble either. I'd tell the following true story:

It began in March of last year, with a phone call home. "I've got great news," I told my wife. Then I proceeded to read from the front page of the newspaper: "The gene that causes Huntington's disease has been discovered after a decade-long search, sparking hope a cure can be found for the deadly neurological disorder." Ramona listened, her heart pounding.

As a young teen she was told that her father had the disease before he died in a drowning accident. The news meant there was a fifty-fifty chance she would eventually die from it. During the next 20 years, she watched three siblings—all in their 30s—contract the disease, one making the slow and humiliating journey to a nursing home.

By the time the newspaper clipping arrived, Ramona had resigned herself to the fact that she had it too. The symptoms were there: depression, lack of sleep, loss of memory, irritability, occasional clumsiness—even a craving for sweets. I kept telling her that each of these could be traced to living with me. This she found amusing for a while, but every time she stumbled, every time she arrived at the fridge and forgot why she was there, she knew she had Huntington's. So each time *I* stubbed my toe, I told her about it. Each time *I* arrived at the fridge and stared blankly at the salad dressing (a daily occurrence), I would inform her. And we would laugh. And sometimes we'd cry.

With the morning paper came the realization that for the first time in history those who were at risk could know their future with a simple blood test.

So two months later we sat together in a cold, sterile laboratory as a nurse took Ramona's blood. Normally I'm not so eager to watch the procedure, but I wanted to make sure they got it right. "There's no chance of the tubes getting mixed up, is there?" I asked, wondering how many times she'd heard that one. The nurse smiled at my worry, then showed us how the tubes were labeled. I appreciated the method. But I had no idea that limited public interest and even less government funding would make us wait ten months for the results.

During those months we were surprised by the comfort of God's promises. On the countless nights when we lay in bed, unable to sleep, Bible verses hidden away in my childhood came back to comfort us. "God is our refuge and strength, an ever present help in trouble. Therefore we will not fear, though the earth give way and the mountains fall into the heart of the sea" (Psalm 46:1). "'For I know the plans I have for you,' declares the Lord . . . 'plans to give you hope and a future'" (Jeremiah 29:11)

Sometimes I'd even sing to her:

When peace like a river attendeth my way,
When sorrow like sea billows roll,
Whatever my lot, Thou hast taught me to say,
It is well, it is well with my soul.

Then I would look over at Ramona. She was usually
asleep. And, almost without exception, she was smiling.

❊❊❊

In early January the phone call came. The waiting was
over. The verdict was in. We would hear it—on February
14. Valentine's Day. *Was this someone's idea of a cruel joke?* I
wondered. *This is a day for cupids and hearts . . . not final ver-
dicts.* Then I realized how fitting it was. You see, when I
stood at the front of a church on August 28, 1982, I said I'd
be her sweetheart no matter what would come our way. In
sickness and in health. Until death separated us. I had little
idea what that meant, but it was a promise I will not break.
And I renewed my vow again as we entered the waiting
room on Valentine's Day.

Another couple joined us. My brother Tim, too. He's a
mature pastor, you know. He told funny stories while we
waited. Perhaps that sounds strange. Insensitive. Irreverent
even. But we had done all the crying. We had spent ten
months on our knees. And so, in the face of certain tears,
we did some first-class laughing. Tim had just reached another punch line when the doctor arrived, looking a little
bewildered. People don't laugh in *this* waiting room.

We wound our way down a corridor and into a dimly lit office. Beside an oak desk sat another doctor. No one was smiling, I noticed. We exchanged nervous greetings. She opened an envelope, examined its contents, and kindly said, "Ramona, you have the normal gene."

A thousand things flashed through my mind during the next few seconds. *She has the disease. The normal Huntington's gene. Our children have a fifty-fifty chance of the same. In ten years the girl I love will be an invalid.* Then the doctor said, "Which means you don't have Huntington's."

There was silence.

"You mean I DON'T have it?" Ramona was on the edge of her chair.

"You don't have it."

"I DON'T?" She was standing now.

"You *don't*."

Next thing we knew we were hugging two doctors and thanking them profusely. Out in the hall, we couldn't remember which way to go. We didn't mind at all.

❊❊❊

You know, when I think of happiness, I think of that moment. Who wouldn't rejoice at such news? Who wouldn't celebrate the removal of a 20-year death sentence?

But if I were asked today about the biggest surprise of my first 32 years on the planet earth, I wouldn't talk about happiness. I'd talk about *joy*. You see, the last ten months could not be described as happy. But strangely, they were jam-packed with joy. Joy doesn't depend on happy endings. On good news or sunny circumstances. Joy comes from knowing that whatever happens, God is good. Whatever happens, God loves me. Whatever happens, we will live forever because of the death sentence God placed on His Son.

Oh yes, you're wondering about Ramona's symptoms. Well, the doctors attribute them to depression, but she's smiling a little more lately. And she finally admits that most of them can be traced to living with me. I'm wondering, though, about the craving for pickles and ice cream.

Peter, Paul, and Barry

WHEN I WAS A KID, I loved playing baseball with the big guys. When I stepped up to the plate, pitchers who ordinarily threw lightning bolts would lob the ball in a gentle rainbow arch. I would quiver and shake and swing somewhere in the general vicinity of the ball. Danny Boutwell, a tall teenager with a foreboding fastball, was particularly merciful. After my feeble swing he'd say, "That's okay, Philip, you try again. Try swinging *after* it leaves my hand this time." Then he'd spit in the dirt and move three steps closer and throw the ball even slower so I could swing once again. "No sweat," he'd say, "you're allowed thirteen strikes."

On occasion, I actually managed to hit the ball, which was an automatic ticket to first base since the infield had gone to sleep. But usually by the sixth or seventh swing, Larry Charter, who played right field, had lost patience and was dancing like an umpire between first and second and yelling: "He's out! He's out!" Danny Boutwell, who was downright imposing on the mound would turn and glare at Larry, then smile and wave me back into the batter's box.

"He's allowed another strike," Danny would say. And he'd lob another one, a big grapefruit that grew riper as it neared home plate. My hands trembled. My knees knocked. And once, on a beautiful day in late May, a day filled with sunshine and the singing of birds and a light breeze blowing towards right field, I smacked that grapefruit—just over Larry's head. As he shuffled shamefully across the gravel road to get it, I rounded the bases, grinning. As I crossed home plate, I looked at Danny. He was grinning, too.

Ah, how I loved playing baseball with the big guys.

✿✿✿

I spoke recently to a group of men. I talked about baseball and I talked about my dad. I think I called the talk "What My Dad Did Right." Afterwards, a man who couldn't have been older than 40 approached me. "Barry" was etched across his name tag. "Thanks," he said. "I needed to laugh today." Then he told me why. "When I hear of 50-year marriages, like your parents have, I want to crawl someplace and hide. I'm on my third one. Where do I go from here?"

I usually think of good answers well after the question, so I breathed a prayer, then said what came to mind: "God can forgive you of yesterday and help you be faithful today." He had tears in his eyes. "I feel like a failure," he said, and walked away.

✿✿✿

I wish I could talk to Barry again. I'd tell him about Danny Boutwell and that gentle pitch from an arm capable of a lightning fastball. I'd tell him about God's mercy.

Then I'd tell him about John Creasey. In his bid to have a book published, John received 753 rejection slips. Yes, 753. He could have wallpapered his home, but John's mind wasn't on interior decorating. Instead, he sent out one more manuscript. The result? The English novelist went on to publish 564 books.

I wish I could tell Barry about Babe Ruth. You see, most sports trivia buffs can tell you that The Babe hit 714 home runs. But few know that he struck out 1,330 times.

Most of all, I'd like to tell Barry that the Bible is full of stories of saints who struck out. I'd tell him about Peter, the disciple who vowed to follow Jesus at any cost, then denied Him with an oath. I'd tell him that Moses stuttered, that Thomas doubted, that Zaccheus didn't measure up, and that Jonah ran into a whale of a time. I'd tell him about David, a guy who liked rooftops. A king who was guilty of adultery and murder, then amazingly enough, referred to as "a man after God's own heart." Why? Because, like Peter and Moses and Thomas and Zacchaeus and Jonah, David knew where to go with his failure. When the prophet Nathan confronted him about his sin, David prayed,

> Have mercy on me, O God, according to your unfailing love; according to your great compassion blot out my transgressions. Wash away all my iniquity and cleanse me from sin . . . Create in me a pure heart, O God, and renew a steadfast spirit within me. Do not cast me from your presence or take your Holy Spirit from me. Restore

to me the joy of your salvation and grant me a willing spirit, to sustain me (Psalm 51:1,2, 10–12).

David found that "God's anger lasts for a moment, but his favor lasts a lifetime" (Psalm 30:5). "Failure doesn't come in the falling," David might say, "It comes in not getting back up."

In the 1992 Olympics, British runner Derek Redmon tore a ligament midway through his race. As the rest of the runners went on to finish, Derek lay on the ground, holding his leg and writhing in pain. For years he had pushed himself toward the goal: Olympic gold. For years he had focused all his energy on one thing: winning. Now those hopes and dreams lay shattered on the track.

Then, amazingly, as television cameras rolled, Derek pushed himself off the ground. As the crowd watched, Derek began to run again, determined to finish the race. But after a few short strides, his legs buckled and he slowed to a walk.

A man appeared on the track then. Security guards tried to stop him, but he was as determined as the runner. Putting his arm around Derek's shoulder, he began coaxing him along. As the crowd thundered its approval, the two crossed the finish line.

The man was Derek's father.

If you're reading this Barry, I hope you'll remember Derek. And I hope you'll remember the words of the apostle Paul:

> But one thing I do: forgetting what lies behind and reaching forward to what lies ahead, I press on toward the goal for the prize of the upward call of God in Christ Jesus (Philippians 3:13,14).

Have your knees buckled lately?

Are your dreams lying in a shattered heap on the track? Perhaps you feel like a little kid standing at home plate, wondering who's calling the strikes. Never forget: God is there with you. He towers above the rest, offering forgiveness and a steady hand.

With His help you can knock this next pitch across the gravel road, and clean out of the ballpark.

Bringing Up Daddy

I made a new rule last night at dinner time. Any complaining about the food and I give the kids another helping. If they say, "Aw, Mom, not tomato soup and beans again," I pour them another spoonful of each. A very generous spoonful. Believe me, the complaining stopped on a dime. But as we neared dessert time, and I pulled the ice cream from the freezer, I noticed a grin on Stephen's face. As I dished out the first helping, I heard him say, "Aw, Dad, not ice cream again! I hate ice cream!" And the others joined him. When we listen to our children, we'll never be short on laughter. And when we listen to our lives, we may even learn a few things, too. Here are a few insights I've picked up from my kids, my spouse—and yes, even my mother-in-law.

CHAPTER
38

Losing My Shirt

I RECALL WELL the day my wife and I first discussed the in-law problem. As a 19-year-old to whom much wisdom had been entrusted, I made it unmistakably clear to my potential wife that in-law is synonymous with trouble. "Should we tie the knot," I said, "we will be marrying *each other,* not any of each other's immediate relatives."

"We will live in different towns, cities, or countries from them," I tactfully continued. "And should one of them choose to move into a town, city, or country which is in or near one which we inhabit, we will distance ourselves with a U-Haul or," and this I voiced most emphatically, "I will eat my blue, pin-striped shirt or possibly a three-piece suit."

She just smiled. And punched me rather hard upside the arm.

One year later, the most surprising thing happened: She agreed to marry me. And following a blissful honeymoon, we found ourselves living in a small town which was quite peaceful and also largely in-law-free.

But as is often the case with those who vow to refrain from eating things like shirts, they inevitably end up chewing upon one, and sometimes even savoring the flavor. In my case, it happened something like this . . .

We had friends who had them. We had seen them in photo albums. At stoplights. In strollers. Besides, it seemed like a good idea at the time. So we decided to have children.

Four years later we became the proud parents of a little boy. We were told we could name him, and so we did. People brought gifts and generally just drooled when they saw him. "He's so cute," they would say sweetly. Then they would look at me, comparing.

"Wow, this child is REALLY cute. How did this child get to be so cute?" Other than that, it was all quite fun. Not so much fun at the outset for Ramona, I'll admit, but nevertheless fun for me.

Several complications set in in the aftermath of labor. For one thing, it became apparent rather quickly that my wife would not be playing beach volleyball for a few weeks, nor would she be cooking or cleaning the house, which until now had been her custom.

"So what's for supper?" she would ask from our waterbed, where she was feeding the youngest member of the household, and longing for some sustenance herself.

"Well . . . ," I said, slamming cupboard doors, "We could have . . . um . . . let's see . . . we could order in some Chinese food."

"Phil," said a voice from the bedroom, "we don't have any money, remember? We spent it on diapers."

"No problem," I said, still slamming cupboards, "I'll boil some water and we can have some . . . uh, what goes good with water?"

"Soup," came the answer.

"My mother fed me nothing but leftover soup for twenty years," I said. "We have never found the original bowl!"

Laughter came from the waterbed. "Don't worry," said she, "someone is coming tomorrow to help you out."

"And who," I questioned, "might that someone be?"

"My mother," said she.

I had heard and exchanged a few hundred mother-in-law jokes, like the one which defines her as a woman who is never outspoken. I knew there was a plant with sharp leaves known as mother-in-law's tongue. But I was altogether unprepared for what would happen to my preconceived notions during the following week.

In the space of a few short days I gained a new appreciation for one who had raised seven children all by herself—after her husband drowned trying to save one of them. Someone whose faith in God had grown through trials I could know little of. "I love mountaintop experiences," she said one day. "But nothing grows on the mountaintop; you have to get down in the valley where the dirt is."

Believe it or not, by the end of the week, I was calling her "Mom." It may have had something to do with her gift of peeling a squealing newborn from the arms of a rookie father and rocking peace and serenity into the home. And I suppose it didn't hurt that twice that week she brought me face to face with some of the best ham and roast beef in the world.

Ah, there's no one in the world quite like Grandma.

Several years have come and gone since my change of heart. And during that time "Mom" has moved where she can now reach us toll-free. In fact, about once a month she cuts my hair. Yes, I know it sounds like the makings for a good episode of *Alfred Hitchcock Presents,* but it is the truth. Once a month I have this strange sensation as the sharp scissors brush close to my ears. What if she knows what I once thought of her? And so those haircuts provide me a monthly lesson in trust. And from her the ultimate display of self-control.

Through the years I have listened to others who have decided to get along without certain members of their families. But I think that's a little like deciding you don't like your left leg and can get along without it. Oh sure, you may learn to walk again, but you will always be missing out on something.

In my case, I wouldn't be the only one missing out. When the grandparents arrive at our house, the children can hardly contain their excitement. They descend from the rafters with squeals of delight to be hugged, baby-sat, read to, and spoiled.

It may have cost me that blue, pin-striped shirt, but I wouldn't want it any other way.

CHAPTER

39

Bearly There

WHEN I BEGAN WRITING BOOKS, I had no idea anyone would want to read them. I thought my mother would buy four copies out of kindness and sympathy, then send them to aunts I had never met. I also had no idea that television shows would call, asking me to come and tell my stories before live audiences. Nothing that happened in high school prepared me for television, with the possible exception of the time I showed up late for English class sporting a rip in my corduroy trousers the exact length of the Mississippi River. I had almost made it to my desk unnoticed when a mean little kid who sat near the front, where he could leave pieces of fruit after class, pointed at my pants, snorted loudly, and began to laugh, causing a ripple effect that picked up speed and volume as it spread across the room like a train coming down the tracks—tracks to which I was tied.

When I was asked to appear on a national morning program, I was, to put it mildly, a little nervous. In fact, I hardly slept thinking about the questions. What if they ask me, "Phil, how do I raise my kids without raising my blood pressure?" and all I can think of is, "Now I lay me down to sleep, I pray Thee, Lord, my soul to keep"? And I fell asleep dreaming of train tracks.

When I begin telling friends about my television appearance (so they will pray for me), I realize that I am not so much nervous as I am proud. After all, none of them have been on TV, except for Harold Leo, who saw himself once while walking past Radio Shack. *Wow, Phil. You're really something,* a voice seems to whisper, *You're going to be on television*. And the whisper pleases my ears.

"Daddy?" Rachael, who should be sleeping, has just tip-toed into my study to say good night. Again.

"Whatcha doing?" she asks, holding down the Z key on my computer. An important paragraph is swirling through my head, and I don't have time for questions.

"I'm writing, Rachael. You're supposed to be in bed."

"Will you play with us tomorrow?"

"No, I have to go away for a few days."

"How long will you be gone?"

"Three sleeps."

"Will you be lonely?"

"I will miss you, Rachael. Good night."

The next day as I pack my suitcase, Jeffrey brings me his stuffed bear. Much of the fur has been loved off. The eyes are not positioned for seeing. But it is Jeffrey's favorite animal. "You might be lonely," he says, handing it to me. "You shall take Heide Bear."

❄❄❄

Airline passengers watch from the corners of their eyes as I take my seat. A grown man with a briefcase and a teddy bear. Hang on to the children, Ethel. He looks unstable. Insecure. Probably needs counseling. They are right. All that's going through my mind is: "Now I lay me down to sleep." I can't even remember the next line.

On the day of the program, Ramona gathers the children to watch. Jeffrey shows special interest: "That's my bear," he says proudly. And, sure enough, there it is. On national television. The hosts jokingly try to pry it away from me, but I hang on for dear life. "My four-year-old was concerned that I'd be lonely," I tell the cameras, "so he gave me his bear."

Jeffrey is excited about his dad being on TV. So excited that he manages to sit still for almost 20 seconds—watching Bear. Then he saunters off down the hallway to build swords with which to poke his big brother.

On the second day, the hostess asks me a tough question: "Phil, what are some practical ways of being a good dad?" I have a very helpful answer in the back of my mind, but that's where it stays. "Well," I say, "it's like Martin Luther once said . . ." and the idea gets wedged somewhere in the back half of my brain and will not come forward. I try again. "Martin Luther once said that . . . um . . . that we should never forget what he said, which was . . . oh, I can't remember." The quote of course comes to me moments after the show. An amazing quote: "My own father was hard, unyielding, and relentless. I can't help but think of God that way." I wanted to tell the audience the importance of grace-full parenting. Of remembering that little children are watching us. That 100 years from now people won't remember the size of our wallets or the brand of our car, but the world could be a better place because we invested in our kids.

That night I fall asleep, a teddy bear resting beside me.

In the darkness of a Sunday morning I leave the hotel for the airport. It's early, but I'm smiling. Who wouldn't smile? The week has been a success. I've appeared on one of the top-rated morning shows in the country. I've spoken several times, made lots of contacts, sold lots of books. I've even received invitations to return. As the plane takes off, the voice no longer whispers. It hollers in my ear: *You're really something, Callaway.* And I like the sound of that voice.

Then, suddenly, the awful truth hits me: Fellow passengers aren't watching me from the corners of their eyes. They are not questioning my sanity. I have my briefcase, but no bear. It's lying on the floor of a hotel room.

As we take off, images flash through my mind. The day my first book was published. After receiving copies in the mail, I proudly rushed it home to show the kids. Rachael held my life's work in her hands and smiled at the cover. Then she set the book down and asked, "Dad, what kind of sparrow is that?" She was looking out the window at the bird feeder. Jeffrey was more interested, though. He picked the book up and chewed on a corner. Thirty percent off.

A few months later I walked to the stage in front of a large gathering to receive a few awards. Stephen was there. He was sitting near the back, and I hoped he could see me. He would be proud, you know. But later I learned that he had been too busy playing Mr. Squishhead with a friend to even notice. They were squeezing their faces at each other, oblivious to my moment in the spotlight.

A movie is showing on a large screen at the front of the plane. I try to watch but the image is blurry. I can't see past the tears. "Lord," I pray, "I've been so caught up with myself lately that I've left some things on the floor. I've been too busy working to play with the kids. Too busy writing to read Your Word. Too busy talking about myself to hear Your voice. Please forgive me."

At home, the children wait. When I walk through the door Rachael greets me with three days' worth of hugs. Stephen wants to show me a castle he's been working on.

Jeffrey just wants his bear.

I sit him down and start my confession. When I finish, he begins to cry. "It's gone?" he says. "You forgot?"

Picking up the phone, I say, "Here, you help me dial. 1 . . . 9 . . ." He is wiping the tears away and poking at the digits . . . 6 . . . 4 . . . "Hello? . . . Yes . . . Could I talk with the manager? . . . Hi . . . I stayed there this weekend and left a small brown bear in my room . . . Huh? . . . You're kidding . . . You're not kidding? . . . Great . . . Here's my address . . ."

A broad smile crosses my face as I hang up the phone. "Guess what? The lady has your bear on her desk. She was looking at it as we talked. Heide Bear is fine. She's going to put it in a nice comfortable box and mail it in the morning."

A week later, Jeffrey thinks it's Christmas.

And now, whenever I travel, Heide Bear comes along. A four-year-old boy won't have it any other way. In fact, I'm writing this chapter in a strange hotel room, but a friendly animal sits atop my briefcase. Her eyesight has worsened. More fur has been loved off. But I wouldn't trade this bear for anything. Oh sure, I receive some strange stares when I board airplanes. And Ethel still rounds up the kids. But I carry with me a small reminder that all the success in the world doesn't compare to the trust of a little child.

A small reminder that those who pursue big dreams must be careful not to leave the little ones behind.

CHAPTER

40

The Great Recession

I DON'T OFTEN purchase magazines at the checkout counter. But on this occasion, surrounded by frenzied shoppers, I couldn't help noticing (right next to Harrison Ford) the smiling faces of several of the most successful movie stars in cinematic history. What really interested me was not their faces but the fact that they were having a problem similar to mine. If I paid the cover price (only $2.95), they would tell me how to fix it.

I first became aware of The Problem while brushing my teeth one night. My wife, who would never say anything to intentionally hurt anyone (me included) was brushing her teeth, too, and standing over me while I rinsed. When I stood up I could tell by the look on her face that she had seen something vitally important. "YOORGOOBLLLD!" she said through a mouthful of toothpaste. After rinsing, she repeated five words that have haunted me ever since:

"Phil, you are going bald!"

This came as no surprise. You do not need the IQ of a nuclear physicist to notice that lately my head is looking more like a mosquito landing zone than the last 10 seconds of a Grecian Formula commercial. I know this. We have mirrors around the house. I am also reminded of The Great Recession whenever my wife and I meet people: "Nice to meet you, Phil. And what did you say your daughter's name was?" But my "daughter" had never actually verbalized the startling truth before: "You are going bald, Phil."

"I know," I said. Then I flicked my toothbrush at her.

If I sound a little sensitive about this issue, it's because I am. I have heard the late-night radio ads. I have seen the infomercials. Both try to make you feel that being bald is as stylish as wearing boots to an opera. But I have also learned that we husbands have few options when it comes to balding. For instance, here are several things we are told to try. None of them work.

1. Comb it differently. When you are young, you adjust your hair to the existing hairstyle. But when you grow old, you are encouraged to adjust your hairstyle to the existing hair. My own father—who went bald back when the earth was flat—did this. The trick here is to grow your hair very long on one side and comb it carefully over the deceased area. This does not work. This does not even fool small children, who will point this out to you perhaps right during church. "HEY, MOM. THERE'S A RAT ON MR. WILSON'S HEAD!" I have also heard it suggested that you grow your eyebrows to their full length and comb them back. I have yet to see this done effectively.

2. Use Minoxidil. Researchers tell us that Minoxidil is the only proven hair-growing drug. "Here, Mr. Callaway, this works on an eight-ball, it should work on you," they say, opening their cash registers. Unfortunately, Minoxidil has side effects. I took some myself, but I can't remember what the side effects are.

3. Try relocating. The basic principle here is simply redistribution: moving hair from an area where it exists to The Dead Zone. This is something you will not want to try at home, but skilled surgeons will be happy to do this for you for $15,000 (I'm not kidding). After approving your VISA card, they will insert individual hairs into pinholes they have made in your head using hypodermic needles. Unfortunately, these little procedures sometimes require years of treatment, and there's a good chance that the hair surrounding the transplant will fall out.

4. Consider classical music. After extensive research, Daiichi Pharmaceutical, a leading Japanese drug maker, is promoting a compact disc of Mozart's music (now available only in pharmacies). The company claims that the music will soothe the listener, relieve stress, and even reverse the balding process. I hope they're on to something there, but I'm skeptical. I have conducted similar research on my father in which I play Eagles compact discs for him. This causes his head to *appear* hairier.

Standing in line with Harrison Ford that day, I reconsidered these four facts, then did what most men would do who are living under a recession: I reached for my wallet and pulled out an extra $2.95.

Upon arriving home, I excitedly turned to page 98, seeking some timely advice. There they were: Bill Murray, Jack Nicholson, Bruce Willis, Ted Danson, Ron Howard, and several others, each of them hiding his baldness behind—you guessed it—a baseball cap. *Hey,* I thought, *so this is the secret? Keep it under your hat?* I was so disappointed that I decided then and there to make a little list of my own.

Here it is:

1. Use your head for something else. When people remind me how bald I am getting, I like to remind them that some people use their hormones for growing hair. I do this as nicely as I can. But the point is, we need to concern ourselves with what's inside our heads, not what's on top.

2. Be content with such hair as thou hast. According to *Details* magazine American men spent close to ten billion dollars last year trying to postpone the inevitable. In so doing they missed out on what is really important. 2 Corinthians 4:16 says, ". . . Though outwardly we are wasting away, yet inwardly we are being renewed day by day." As I grow older, I trust my wife will enjoy my company more because I am content with whom God has made me. Content because of what He has given me. Content because of what He is doing inside my head.

So, men, I hope you've benefited from this advice. If it doesn't work, go ahead and put your hat on. Should that fail, I have one more suggestion: Brush your teeth alone.

CHAPTER

41

Fit to Be Tired

WHEN RAMONA AND I were first married, she worked at a pharmacy for five dollars an hour and I was a stay-at-home mooch. Jobless for almost a month, I learned to play the drums, and found my calling there and decided to enter the recording industry so that others might be touched by a gift that had taken me completely by surprise. One night Ramona came home from work exhausted and hollered, "WHAT'S THAT NOISE? ARE YOU KILLING CHICKENS IN THERE?" and, in so doing, shattered my illusions of grandeur. I decided that night to look around for other hobbies and before long, found one.

On weekends I began videotaping weddings, a hobby that bore handsome financial rewards. Usually the bride's father, who looked extremely exhausted, would hand me a check and say, "Here, you fill in the amount . . . it doesn't much matter now." Only once did I feel guilty for taking his money. Only once did I consider paying him for the entertainment. This was the time the groom fainted dead

away and fell on a candle. His hair caught fire instantly, and
the poor guy woke up looking as if he were wondering
whether or not the bride fanning him with the pastor's
sermon notes was someone he wanted to spend the rest of
his life with. All in all, I watched the start of more than 100
weddings in ten years, and to this day you could not pay
me three million dollars to tape one more. Thankfully the
majority of those marriages are intact, but every once in a
while I hear of another one that has caught fire and I feel
nothing but sadness and find myself wondering what they
will do with my tape. It's not easy for me to watch high
fidelity go the way of the eight-track, particularly in
Christian homes where perhaps a Third Party should be
consulted more often.

I myself come from a long line of married people, who
must have decided at some point to stick together when
the spark was gone. My parents, for instance, have been
married 57 years despite the fact that my father still clips
his toenails in the living room.

Not long ago, I asked Mom and Dad what made their
marriage last, and without skipping a beat on his pace-
maker, Dad said, "Senility. I wake up each morning and I
can't remember who this old girl is. So each day is a new
adventure."

"No, I'm serious," I said. "Give us five good reasons
you're still together." It was an unusual pop quiz, compli-
cated somewhat by three grandchildren who were clamor-
ing for their attention.

"I'll tell you what," said Mom, removing our youngest
son's index finger from her ear, "give us a little time. I'll
write them out for you."

The next morning she dropped by and handed me a note. "You wouldn't show this to anyone, would you?" she asked. "I don't want people to think it's the final word on marriage."

I smiled. "You know me, Mom. I wouldn't dream of it."

FIVE REASONS WE'RE STILL TOGETHER
by Victor and Bernice Callaway

1. Example.   When we were married, we hardly knew about divorce. We didn't know any divorced people. I guess everyone at our wedding, including us, fully expected the knot to stay tied. We had watched their marriages. We had seen their faithfulness. We would stay faithful, too. We realize you won't have that advantage, son. Some of your closest friends may pack it in. But no matter how dark the road gets, you will find bright examples of faithfulness. And when you can't find examples, you can still *be* one.

2. Commitment.   Sometimes I felt like walking out on Dad. And a few times I did. Early in our marriage I occasionally took long walks to get away from him. But I always returned to his loving arms. We made a pledge before God that we would stay committed to each other for life.

3. Devotions.   Through reading God's Word and praying together almost every night, we learned what God planned and expected for our marriage. We memorized verses that encouraged us to be loving, kind, and honest, and to keep on forgiving. We asked God for guidance, and He provided it. We prayed for children and embraced each one of them as gifts from God.

4. Togetherness. As a Christian family we stuck together, warts and all. Though we often failed, we are learning to admit wrong and ask for forgiveness. We laughed lots. We cried lots. We talked lots. We worked together and we played together.

5. Goals. Since the day we said our vows, our goal has been to walk worthy of the Lord and to keep on walking until we see His face. Sometimes we've fallen flat on our faces, but we've been given grace to get up and claim God's promise: "My presence shall go with you, and I will give you rest." Aging brings with it a whole new challenge. It is no flat plateau; sometimes the hills seem steeper and the cliffs more precarious, but we are learning to trust God for what's ahead and to thank Him for the abundant and undeserved mercies of the past.

The other day someone informed me that another of my videotapes had become obsolete, and I thought of Mom and Dad. When they stood at the altar, the temperature had dipped to 45 below in Toronto, Ontario, Canada. There was no video camera humming, no photographer present, and they had no guarantees. They knew that ten days later Dad would go back to war, leaving his tearful bride waving from a train station platform. So they joined hands and promised to be faithful. They had no idea that their second child would die in their arms or that they would spend their entire lives below the poverty line. But they vowed to comfort each other, no matter what came their way.

By today's standards Mom and Dad didn't have much. Just 75 dollars, a solitary wedding ring, and a suitcase full of dreams. Half a century later, they still don't have much. Just an antique clock and a Ford Tempo that sometimes runs. But their dreams were never about good fortune. Instead they dreamed of children who would follow God—and they got five of them. They dreamed of years of faithfulness—and they got 57 of them. You can travel the world, but I'll guarantee you one thing: You'll never meet two wealthier people.

By the way, Mom did give me permission to reprint the note. And as she did, she reminded me of a few final cliches: "Even when you're 70 you have to work at marriage," and "It's never over till it's over." Then she said with a twinkle, "I think we're pretty safe, though. Dad may be senile, but I've grown too old to run away from him."

CHAPTER

42

Picture Perfect?

"**M**Y GREATEST ACHIEVEMENT," wrote Sir Winston Churchill, "was convincing my wife to marry me." I agree completely. But at times I think my greatest achievement is convincing my wife to *keep* me.

It's been 17 years since we said our vows, since we promised God and a few hundred witnesses that death would be the only thing that would separate us. A few times since Ramona has thought of killing me, I'm sure, but she insists that I'm safe. "Besides," she smiles, "we don't have any arsenic around here anyway." On our seventeenth wedding anniversary she almost started looking for some, though.

We had spent a wonderful morning together, gazing into each other's eyes over a Continental breakfast. And in the heat of the morning I made a deadly mistake. I suggested we go shopping together. Now 17 years have taught me some things. One of them is that you should not walk downstairs in the darkness when your children have been playing with small trucks. Another is that my wife and I are completely incompatible when it comes to shopping malls. Whereas I like record stores and stereo shops, Ramona prefers anything that spells "Clothing: 50 percent off," and "No payments till January." As you might suspect, she welcomed my suggestion and by noon we found ourselves staring at acres of furniture and appliances under fluorescent lights—which are designed by scientists to slowly drive husbands berserk and to the brink and over the edge, to the point where they will reach for their wallets and say things like, "No problem" and "Whatever you want, Dear, it's really up to you."

For some time we had been discussing the purchase of a picture for a blank wall in our dining room, and that day as we walked the acres I finally found the perfect one. Framed in forest green, this masterpiece combined diverse influences such as Rembrandt and Thomas Kinkade in a peaceful breakfast scene, begging the viewer to enter the scene and partake of breads and fruits and juices. "Put me in your dining room," the picture said to me. And I promised I would.

The picture did not speak to my wife. She found it distasteful, too large for the wall, and she gently told me so. She had picked out a picture of her own, one which fit our dining room in every way. It's called "Fleurs sur la Terrace," a famous French breakfast scene. I said something I shouldn't have when she showed it to me. I don't think it's important that I tell you my exact words, but essentially they went like this: "Whatever. You always get your own way regardless." Ramona went through the checkout stand early that day, and quite quickly. Then she sat in the van and looked straight ahead.

The scene reminded me of another anniversary. One which took place exactly nine years earlier . . .

※※※

"Hollywood Stars Falling Out of Love."

The bold headline jumps out at me from a tabloid known worldwide for its desperate pursuit of truth, accuracy, integrity, and particularly freedom of speech. Below is a celebrity couple in happier days. The caption reads: " . . .We just don't love each other anymore." At the top of the page is perhaps the only truth gracing this ignominious publication—the date: August 28.

Ah, now I remember why I am standing in line surrounded by close-ups of Harrison Ford. I am here to purchase an anniversary card. Yes, as of today, Ramona and I have been married 2,920 days. This afternoon we will celebrate with a round of golf and then dinner alone. I can't wait!

※※※

"You spent *how much* on *what?*"

Little time has passed since our romantic candlelight dinner and disastrous round of golf. I am standing in the living room, hands on my hips, trying my best to look imposing.

"Forty-nine dollars on clothes."

"FORTY-NINE DOLLARS! Why didn't you tell me?" I sound angry. Angrier than I am.

"I did, but you were too busy reading." She is right. I remember now.

"Uh . . . well . . ." My hands are off my hips, and I am fumbling for a reply. "I just think that's a lot to spend on clothes right now."

"Pardon me?" Her voice is growing louder. Soon neighbors will gather. "You buy things like stereos and cars and I can't even buy some clothes? Which were ON SALE?" she adds.

"I didn't say that. I just think we need to be a little more careful right now. We just had holidays, and you know we needed that car, and . . ."

As things heat up I realize that she is right. But there's no way I'm admitting it today.

It is time for a walk. Down the street I smile and wave at a neighbor, but I am severely miffed. "Sometimes arguing with your wife is like trying to blow out a light bulb," I muse. "Especially when you're wrong."

"How are you doing, Phil?"

"Fine, thank you. Just fine," I am smiling at my neighbor. And lying.

What I'd really like to say is this: "Okay. So I haven't been easy to live with lately. But I'm not that bad. I don't drink our money away. Or beat her. Maybe I feel this way because I don't love her anymore. Ha. It's like those Hollywood stars. Maybe our old candle has undergone burnout, too. Oh, sure. I'll stay with her. But I won't speak to her ever again. We'll live together. In silence. You see, I don't think I'm in love anymore."

And so, that night, for the first time in more than eight years of married life, I let the sun go down on our wrath. It is not an easy thing I do, but let's face it: Of all the sins we commit, anger is undoubtedly the most fun.

Early the next morning she is sleeping when I leave for work. Smooth sailing. My vow of silence is intact.

But in the office there is trouble of another kind. My assignment for the day is to write an article for a marriage magazine. An article on reconciliation. Tell me, how does one write an honest and vulnerable article on marriage when he is mad at his wife?

Picking up my Bible, I begin reading the assigned verses. The book is Colossians and the text seems larger and clearer than any tabloid headline: "Clothe yourselves with compassion, kindness, humility, gentleness and patience. Bear with each other and forgive whatever grievances you may have against one another. Forgive as the Lord forgave you. And over all these virtues put on love, which binds them all together in perfect unity" (Colossians 3:12-14).

Ouch.

Put on love. Not *feel* love, but choose to *do* it.

"Lord," I pray, "I'll need Your help. I'm tired of loving on my own."

Putting down my Bible I pick up the phone. "Honey? Ya, it's me. I . . . I'm sorry. *I was wrong.*"

That evening things are different. We talk long into the night. We speak of love. Not an emotion. Not something we fall into. Or out of. But something we decide to do, whether we feel like it or not.

The next morning I am tired, but there is a smile on my face. An honest smile. It is a good start for a husband with such a long way to go.

🧍🧍🧍

Nine years have passed. Clearly I still have a lot to learn. About things like selflessness and tenderness and holding my tongue. The other day on the way home from shopping for a picture, I said sorry once again. And for the four hundred and eighty-ninth time in 17 years, Ramona forgave me.

Tonight, as we sit around the dinner table together I realize that I am a happy man. I am surrounded by a loving family, smiling at a forgiving wife. There is ample food on our table and no arsenic in my root beer. I'm even starting to enjoy the picture hanging on our dining room wall.

43

Help! It's Raining Relatives!

SOMETIMES GOD SPEAKS to us in the unexpected. An earthquake. A thunderstorm. A flat tire on the way to play bingo. And sometimes if we listen carefully enough, He may even speak to us at a family reunion.

I wasn't going to attend ours this year. I had other plans. Plans to go fishing. Plans for peace, tranquility, and bass. Such virtues have not always been characteristic of my wife's family reunions. This clan gets together and it spells trouble. Thirty people under one roof swapping tales of mischief, and laughing until they need oxygen. When I shared my feelings with Ramona, she had some feelings of her own. "I grew up with these people," she said. "You go fishing and you might as well just take your parka and stay the winter." So, after a long walk and much prayer, I decided to take her advice.

I'm kidding here, of course. If the truth be known, I can't think of a better bunch of people to spend the weekend with. And I'm not just saying this so they will keep me in their wills. I'm saying it because it's true.

On Thursday night the relatives began arriving. They came by the carload carrying large photo albums. There was hugging. Laughing. Picture-taking. And . . . did I mention the hugging? We guys stood around talking about golf and the rainy weather. The ladies took more pictures, planned our Friday, then hugged each other repeatedly.

Late that night, as darkness came down, the rain picked up. "Maybe we should call off the reunion," I suggested, standing at a window squinting at the sky. "I think I hear someone building an ark."

"Very funny," said Ramona, putting an arm around me. I looked down. And noticed that there were tears in her eyes.

"Was it something I said?"

"No," she replied, "I'd just like to . . . can we pray together? I need to talk to God."

Staring at the clouds, she reminded me of some things we'd been trying to forget. Expensive tickets for tomorrow night's Passion Play. An outdoor performance that a week of rain was washing away. "I've been looking forward to this for months," she said. "I want my family to see this play so badly . . . the story of Jesus . . . His miracles . . . His resurrection."

I didn't need to ask why.

A generation ago, Huntington's disease had invaded her family, making death a way of life. The skies, once bright and blue, were clouded with uncertainty now. One after another, three siblings had been diagnosed. "Only God knows how many reunions we have left . . . down here," she said, taking my hand. "I want this one to be memorable." Then she prayed aloud for her brother

Dennis, who lies in a nursing home, curled up in the fetal position. For her two sisters who had come to the reunion, that their bright personalities would keep shining past the ravages of an awful disease. And she prayed for sunny skies. I listened. But, I must admit, my faith was smaller than those drops of rain pelting the window.

Friday morning dawned warm and hot and sunny.

In Florida.

But in Alberta, Canada, the rain was now a torrent. Four inches in two days. A record, someone said. Ramona prayed again at breakfast and at lunch. The skies opened wider. That afternoon we piled into our canoes (I'm exaggerating here) and drove to the nearby town of Drumheller. "I guess this is what they mean by a carpool," I told my wife. She didn't say anything. So I decided I'd lighten the atmosphere with a good joke.

"People in Alberta don't suntan," I said, "they rust."

No one laughed. Not a soul. I turned the windshield wipers higher and tried some others. Like these:

- At least we won't have to water our lawn this year. We'll just drain it.
- We have a water shortage. It's only up to our knees.
- What is the population of Alberta? Four million umbrellas.
- We had a short summer this year. It came on June 8.

They smiled and patted me on the shoulder. "That's okay," they said. "You'll get over it."

We finally docked our canoes at the Royal Tyrell Museum, known worldwide for its huge collection of dead dinosaurs. For 20 bucks the whole family can view the remains and listen to lifeless speeches. After an hour this is about as exciting as watching cheese mold. So I gathered the kids around and made up a speech of my own: "Sixty kajillion years ago (give or take a few months), this Thingasaurus used to roam the hills, eating insects and tomatoes and small children. In fact, that's how they achieved extinction. They kept eating their kids." Then I made frightening noises and chased the children with my claws outstretched.

At six o'clock we exited the museum through the gift shop (convenient, isn't it?). And I couldn't believe it: The sun had poked through.

Ramona didn't seem so surprised. "I knew it," she said, a wide smile spreading across her face.

A few miles from the dinosaur bones we sat in a natural amphitheatre, the sun warming our backs, our umbrellas unopened. For three hours the sky held back. For three hours we watched the story of Jesus unfold. We saw Him offend the Pharisees. Laugh with children. Comfort Mary Magdelene. And we watched in horror as they bolted Him to a cross. The angels turned their backs. The crowd at the foot of the cross jeered and walked away.

Then . . . He took the world by surprise.

On either side of me sat my wife's two sisters. Women, who, along with their husbands and children, desperately longed for healing. But it hit me that night that they had something far better. They had hope. A hope you will not find in a museum filled with bones, but in a place where the tomb is empty. In the simple story of a passionate Savior who died to heal the world.

In the parking lot, Jeffrey noticed my solemn face. "I saw Peter backstage," he said. "He was smoking a cigarette." We laughed out loud together. "If any of the disciples would be smoking a cigarette," I said, "it would be Peter."

On the way home, the sky opened once again, and the rain descended. But we didn't mind. As I punched the cruise control a car passed us, its license plate bearing the one word that best summed up our day: HOPE.

"Look," I said to Ramona. And she did.

"You glad you didn't go fishing?" she asked, with a twinkle in her eye.

"I sure am," I said. "I'd choose a family reunion any day." Then I added, "Would you mind praying about tomorrow? I'd sure like to go golfing."

About the Author

PHIL CALLAWAY is an award-winning columnist and a popular speaker at conferences, churches, camps, and Promise Keepers events. The author of six books, including *Making Life Rich Without Any Money* and *Who Put the Skunk in the Trunk (Learning to Laugh When Life Stinks!)*, Phil's writings have been translated into languages such as Spanish, Polish, Chinese, and English—one of which he speaks fluently. His five-part video series, *The Big Picture,* has been circulated in thousands of churches worldwide. Phil is married to his high school sweetheart, Ramona, and lives in Alberta, Canada, with his three children (his wife lives there, too). For more information on his books, tapes, videos, or speaking ministry, check out his web site at **www.philcallaway.ab.ca** or write P.O. Box 4576, Three Hills, AB TOM 2NO. Phone: 403-443-5511. E-mail: phil.callaway@pbi.ab.ca.

Servant Magazine

Phil is editor of *Servant,* an award-winning magazine read in 101 countries. A ministry of Prairie Bible Institute, *Servant* is full of insightful interviews with well-known Christians, helpful articles, world news, and Phil's trademark humor. For a complimentary one-year subscription, please call 1-800-221-8532, check out the web site **pbi.ab.ca/servant**, or send e-mail to servant@pbi.ab.ca. You can also write:

Servant Magazine
Box 4000
Three Hills, AB Canada
TOM 2NO

Other Good
Harvest House Reading

MAKING LIFE RICH WITHOUT ANY MONEY
by *Phil Callaway*

With humor and candor, award-winning storyteller Phil Callaway shows readers how to find the happiness of a millionaire on the salary of a servant. Truly wealthy people enjoy laughter, simplicity, forgiveness, and hope—whether they have money or not.

WHERE ROOTS GROW DEEP
by *Bob Welch*

In his latest book, Bob Welch offers memorable and moving true stories, written with humor and rich insight that show how critical it is to leave a legacy of life for our children and for generations to come. It's never too late, he writes, to begin creating that legacy. The best time to plant a tree was 20 years ago. The second-best time is now.

SWEETER THAN HONEY
by *Annette Smith*

Her first collection of stories, *The Whispers of Angels,* became a word-of-mouth favorite among Christian readers. Now Annette Smith turns her incredible writing talent from hospital rooms and doctors' offices to the front porches and backyards of her neighborhood, offering wry, insightful looks at the caring, compassion, and craziness of small town life.

BEYOND THE PICKET FENCE
by *Lori Wick*

Wick brings her vibrant faith and romantic heart to these delightful stories about camping in the wilds, celebrating Christmas, finding "first" love, and more. These enchanting and lively snapshots of faith will capture your heart.